THE BATTLE FOR TAIWAN

THE BATTLE FOR TAIWAN

JONAS PARELLO-PLESNER

The battle for Taiwan

The battle for Taiwan
by Jonas Parello-Plesner

2023

Cover: Bettina Kjærulff-Schmidt
Graphic design: Jeanette Bech

Content

Preface to the English edition

This book was published in Danish in August 2023. The author has translated and edited it for the English version removing examples prima relevant to Danish readers.

The book is an easy-read introduction to why the Battle for Taiwan is everybody's concern. It draws on the author's experiences as a diplomat on the EU-China-US beat, think tank scholar and democracy defender over the last two decades, and on his recent conversations in Taiwan staying there between November 2022 and January 2023.

The book addresses the generally interested reader who wants to understand the importance of Taiwan and how a conflict in the Taiwan-Strait holds global significance both economically, militarily and for what values will dominate the 21st Century.

CHAPTER 1

Conflict between Taiwan, China and the USA

The handshake is not as firm as I expect. In fact, it's somewhat limp, but the man is awe-inspiring. His lips are wide and locked in an inscrutable smile that can be read as both arrogant and indulgent. I lean towards the first option. I'm facing Xi Jinping, the undisputed leader of 1.4 billion Chinese and General Secretary of the Communist Party. He has several top members of the Politburo—China's ruling body—with him. However, they huddle behind the great leader. It is unambiguously Xi who wields the baton from start to finish.

Why am I there shaking hands with China's leader? I am part of Danish Prime Minister Lars Løkke Rasmussen's delegation. The meeting is not taking place in China, but in Washington DC at the Omni Shoreham hotel in the spring of 2016. Both Xi Jinping and Lars Løkke Rasmussen are invited by President Barack Obama to the Nuclear Security Summit. I am Lars Løkke Rasmussen's so-called sherpa for the Summit, although I am not, like a Nepalese sherpa, carrying the baggage. It's diplomatic jargon for chief negotiator.

I got the soft handshake from the leader of the Middle Kingdom. But when Xi talks about Taiwan, it is with an iron fist. Even to a Danish prime minister. Xi refers to Taiwan as "the core of Chinese core interests". Therefore, Xi Jinping's handshake is markedly tougher towards Taiwan. Xi Jinping's prestige project is to incorporate Taiwan into the People's Republic of China, a so-called reunification. This term is used widely even though the People's Republic of China and the Communist Party in Beijing have never had control over Taiwan, where the Republic of China, also known as Taiwan, has existed independently since 1949.

From Beijing's corridors of power, the narrative is that there is only one China, and Taiwan is an inseparable part of it. This is the essence of the one-China principle. What Beijing is offering Taiwan is to join China under the "one country, two systems" model. This is the model that Hong Kong also operates under, but where the Communist Party has nevertheless expanded its power and curtailed freedom.

A so-called reunification can be enforced by military force if necessary. The People's Republic of China passed a law in 2005 authorizing a military attack if Taiwan declares independence.

Unlike Xi Jinping, President Tsai Ing-wen is democratically elected in Taiwan. She won the presidential election in 2016 and again in January 2020. Tsai is Taiwan's first female president. She is well-educated with a PhD and loves cats and nature. Her government was the first country in Asia to allow same-sex marriage. In democracy surveys, Taiwan ranks among the top ten in the world. The contrast to Xi Jinping and his authoritarian model could not be greater.

The same contrast applies to my own encounter. I shake hands with President Tsai Ing-wen in January 2023 in the red presidential building in downtown Taipei. Her handshake is firm, actually firmer than Xi's. Her smile seems friendly without arrogance and her eyes are framed by a pair of light glasses. Based on my own handshake barometer, there's a clear winner!

THE WORLD'S MOST DANGEROUS CONFLICT

The relationship between China and Taiwan has the potential for conflict to such an extent that the leading magazine The Economist has put Taiwan on its cover as the most dangerous place in the world because the conflict could trigger a great power war between the US and China. And because conflict over Taiwan could bring the global economy to a standstill. For that reason alone, the future of Taiwan should be of concern to every peace-loving person in the world.

Just as President Vladimir Putin is creating his version of history with the war in Ukraine, Xi Jinping is fighting for "Taiwan as an inseparable part of China's territory and that China has indisputable sovereignty over Taiwan", as the policy line is in Beijing.

Xi Jinping has tasked the Chinese military to prepare its capabilities work for conducting a military invasion. 2027 has been set as the target date. This does not mean that there will automatically be an armed conflict that year, but simply that the Chinese military must have done their homework. The final decision on the timing is Xi Jinping's.

The stakes are high for Xi Jinping. If he succeeds in annexing Taiwan, it will secure his place in history among the leaders of the Chinese Communist Party. And it will secure China a leading place in the world order at the expense of the US. But Xi has also seen how a semi-failed invasion like Putin's in Ukraine can also erode one's position of power.

But what is certain is that Xi does not have as much patience as his predecessor, Chairman Mao, who in 1971, in a conversation with US National Security Advisor Henry Kissinger, said that China could wait 100 years for a solution to the Taiwan question. Instead, Xi states that a solution to the Taiwan issue cannot be passed on from "generation to generation". Xi Jinping appears determined to push through the incorporation of Taiwan during his reign and lifetime. This points to some fateful decisions within the next decade.

While international attention in both August 2022 and April 2023 was focused on Russia's war in Ukraine, China showed its military teeth. In both instances, the Chinese military conducted the most extensive exercises in decades around Taiwan with planes, ships and missiles. Both were Chinese reactions to then Speaker of the US House of Representatives Nancy Pelosi's visit to Taiwan in August 2022, and in April 2023 to the Taiwanese president meeting with then Speaker Kevin McCarthy in the United States.

In practice, the Chinese exercises were practice runs for a military blockade of Taiwan. And a precursor to war. Fortunately, both times it remained an exercise. Just as we saw Russia's military conduct military exercises along the Ukrainian border prior to the Ukraine war. Then, one day in February 2022, it turned real.

In the face of China's military might, the people of Taiwan stand on the frontline. An overwhelming majority of the population does not want to be incorporated into China. If attacked, many Taiwanese hope to draw on the same military and popular resistance as the brave people of Ukraine against a militarily much stronger power.

Behind Taiwan and further out in the Pacific Ocean resides the US Navy and military power. A Chinese attack on Taiwan could be the start of a great power conflict—also of an intensity not seen since World War II. This is different from the Ukraine war, where the US supports Ukraine solely through military assistance. Here, the situation on Taiwan is different, where the US has supplied weapons for decades, but could also be expected to intervene militarily.

"Yes," replies US President Joe Biden on May 23, 2022 in Tokyo in response to a press question about whether the US will defend Taiwan. Until now, the great powers have kept each other in check.

Putin's attack on Ukraine underlines that autocratic leaders can make risky decisions and start wars through invasion. Could Xi Jinping be tempted to embark on a similar war adventure, even if China and the world would suffer in lost lives and economic prosperity?

A military clash in Asia over Taiwan would shake the foundations of the international order—in terms of values, military, technology and economics.

We live with the consequences of the war in Ukraine in European homes through expensive energy and gas bills especially in 2022. But the relationship with China and Taiwan is far more significant for us and the global economy. Even though Taipei is over 8,000 km from Brussels, much further away than Ukraine, we would feel the consequences of a conflict immediately. Economically and technologically on a much larger scale.

Why? Because Taiwanese companies are world leaders when it comes to producing top-of-the-line advanced computer chips. Hiding behind the acronym TSMC, Taiwan Semiconductor Manufacturing Corporation, lies one of the world's most important companies. Their chips are the backbone—but also the stumbling block—of technological globalization.

Without these chips, we would soon run out of iPhones, cars, laptops, microwaves, PlayStations and a whole host of other electronic products.

Similarly, Made in China products are filling up European households. Our supply chains are largely routed through China. 40 percent of the EU's trade in goods passes through the Taiwan Strait according to an analysis by the Central European Institute of Asian Studies. Globalization and the flow of goods as we know them today will be irrevocably changed by conflict. An analysis from Nikkei Asia, a Japanese media outlet, suggests that a Taiwan conflict would cut the global economy by up to 2.6 trillion US dollars. This is equivalent to the entire economy of Italy -a member of the group of the world seven largest economies, the G7.

If China attacked Taiwan, the Danish Prime Minister—along with other European leaders—could expect a call from Washington to impose economic sanctions, just as we have done against Russia after the invasion of Ukraine. Such sanctions would require far greater economic sacrifices from us and our businesses. China's economy is ten times larger than Russia's and is far more interconnected with the rest of the global economy. Similarly, Taiwan is ten times more important in the global economy—because of computer chips—than Ukraine.

There will also be pressure from the other direction. From Beijing. Just as Putin employs gas pipelines as war leverage, China will use its economic muscle to threaten Denmark and Europe. China's strategy will be to pressure other countries to remain neutral in the conflict. The Beijing message to Germany, for example, could sound like this: "If you want to continue selling German cars, chemicals and machinery in China, stay out of this." And in that case, the Germans will face a dilemma between economics and values. China is Germany's biggest market for cars, even bigger than the US.

However, there is much more at stake than economic turbulence. In the big picture, the current world order and the United States' leading role are at stake in a conflict over Taiwan. The outcome of a conflict could determine whether we will continue to live in a freedom-based, liberal world order with the US as the leading power. Or whether China now leads. With its authoritarian values.

If Xi succeeds in invading Taiwan, the alternative is bleak. In early February 2022, Xi Jinping and Putin signed a joint manifesto, the autocrats' international playbook. Russia's invasion of Ukraine has only reinforced that joint vision and cooperation. The two leaders are united in their ambition to diminish US power and to advance their own, what they in more neutral language refer to as a multipolar world order.

In April 2023, Xi Jinping went to Moscow and visited Putin, even though Russia's leader was simultaneously being indicted for war crimes at the International Criminal Court. The cooperation between the two autocrats gives us a scary glimpse of a future world of Chinese dominance, where the yuan replaces the dollar, and where technological surveillance and systematic suppression of individual rights is the basic norm.

After a takeover of Taiwan, the Chinese navy and military can extend its military power further out into the Pacific unhindered. China can be expected to do as it pleases with smaller neighboring countries such as Vietnam, Malaysia and the Philippines in the South China Sea. Japan and South Korea will be under pressure in the next tier. US power will be weakened in Asia, but also globally. The world as we know it will be replaced by one where the strong nation has more rights than the small. The international legal order will be replaced by divisions in spheres of interest around large countries like China and Russia.

That's why the battle for Taiwan's democracy is a story every European and global citizen should know.

MY OWN CHINA AND TAIWAN STORY

In 2005, as an aspiring Danish diplomat, I was given team responsibility for managing Denmark's relations with China. The mood was optimistic. In December 2001, China had joined the World Trade Organization (WTO). This led to a steady increase in trade with all countries in the following years. Both the Danish business community and we at the Ministry of Foreign Affairs saw great opportunities in this development. I was also impressed by China's growth miracle.

At the time, China's reforms looked like they could lead to a more open, rights-based society. In the Danish Ministry of Foreign Affairs, we supported projects with new forms of elections at village level that would give room for independent forces beyond the Communist Party. During those years, China's leaders talked our ears off about how peaceful China's development was. I, too, was listening.

In 2008, I was a lead negotiator on the Danish-Chinese Comprehensive Strategic Partnership and participated in then Prime Minister Anders Fogh Rasmussen's visit to Beijing, where handshakes with Hu Jintao and Wen Jiabao sealed the partnership.

In relation to Taiwan, I was raised with the official One-China policy. To be on the safe side as diplomats, we avoided contact with Taiwan and its representatives as much as possible.

The first time I visited Taiwan myself was in 2009—much later than my many visits to China.

Times seemed more peaceful back then. In 2008, Taiwan's citizens elected Ma Ying-jeou of the Nationalist Party as president. Throughout his term until 2016, he sought to bring Taiwan closer to China. Perhaps the two sides would find a solution themselves, just as Hong Kong—at the time—operated with its own freer system under the "one country-two systems" model. In hindsight, that was naïve thinking.

After resigning from the Ministry of Foreign Affairs in 2009, I started visiting Taiwan. I worked on European Union-China relations for the European think tank European Council on Foreign Relations (ECFR) until 2013.

It was also during those years that my positive understanding of the People's Republic of China steadily declined. In 2010, I saw how fiercely the Chinese regime reacted to the poet Liu Xiaobo winning the Nobel Peace Prize. There was an empty chair in Oslo because Xiaobo was in Chinese prison.

In 2011, I was the target of a Chinese recruitment attempt while I was in Beijing. I was proposed by representatives of the Chinese intelligence service to write positive articles about China in international media in exchange for so-called researcher payment. "No thanks." The Chinese efforts achieved the opposite. I have since written about the experience, to the warning of others, in the New York Times, American Interest and Berlingske. Since then, my articles, which I write regularly for Danish and international press, have only become even more critical of China.

From 2013 to 2017, I returned to diplomatic life and became head of department for foreign policy at the Embassy of Denmark in Washington. Under President Obama, the US had begun its pivot or rebalance towards Asia to match China.

Those years provided a unique insight into the engine room of US China policy and the emerging great power competition that dominates the news headlines today.

The time in Washington provided further contacts and understanding of Taiwan. Even with a one-China policy in place, contacts with Taiwan are much more frequent in the US than in Europe.

In China, Xi Jinping had come to power the year before—in 2012. Unlike his predecessors Hu Jintao and Wen Jiabao, Xi unequivocally perceived democracy and freedoms as dangerous ideas to be countered inside China's borders and beyond. During his first decade in power, repression and surveillance of Chinese civil society increased, independent defense lawyers were purged. In Xinjiang, the Muslim minority Uighurs were placed in inhumane re-education camps. Behind the economic growth miracle, the raw power of the Communist Party and Xi Jinping reign supreme.

In the spring of 2018, I was back in the think tank community at the Hudson Institute in Washington DC, and I got the opportunity to join the French Navy on the warship Dixmude as it sailed through the South China Sea. I wrote about the experience for the Wall Street Journal and the American Interest. Here, too, in the waters south of Taiwan, there is a risk of conflict. China views the entire sea including uninhabited reefs as its rightful property, even though the International Law of the Sea does not back up China's claims. Neighboring countries Vietnam and the Philippines oppose China's claims. Taiwan also has possession of an island in the South China Sea.

China disregards the claims of its neighbors and the international law of the sea in the area. Therefore, the French Navy reserves the right of free navigation and passage, as does the United States. However, the Chinese Navy does not agree.

Our sailing by the disputed Spratly Islands was met by several Chinese frigates. I listened in on Chinese navy-to-navy calls, strictly informing the French ships that we were in Chinese territorial waters. In fact, we were hundreds of kilometers from the Chinese mainland and much closer to the Philippines, Indonesia or Vietnam.

These frigates are just a small part of China's massive naval buildup. It is estimated that China will reach 400 ships by 2025—the world's largest fleet according to the Pentagon's annual assessment. As a French naval officer explained to me while sailing in the South China Sea, China builds the equivalent of France's entire fleet approximately every four to five years.

It is an uncertain time to be a small neighbor of China—also at sea. That was confirmed by my first-hand encounter with China's massive naval build-up. All previous illusions about China's peaceful rise were thoroughly shaken out of me.

Since 2018, I have led the daily work of the Alliance of Democracies Foundation with Anders Fogh Rasmussen as founder and chairman of the board. We work with democratic forces across the globe which include both Hong Kong democracy activists and Chinese dissidents. In Taiwan, we work with the Taiwan Foundation for Democracy and bring in voices from government and civil society.

Among Taiwanese speakers from civil society and government, we had Taiwanese President Tsai Ing-wen speak virtually at the Copenhagen Democracy Summit. This is our annual summit by the Foundation. The Summit is held in Skuespilhuset in Copenhagen and aims to strengthen cooperation between the world's democracies.

Prior to each Copenhagen Democracy Summit, China's embassy in Copenhagen protested about Tsai Ing-wen's attendance both publicly with threatening press releases and to the Ministry of Foreign Affairs behind closed doors. In 2020, the Chinese protests gained extra force because the then sitting US Secretary of State, Mike Pompeo, was on the list of speakers alongside the Taiwanese president.

Taiwanese participation at the conference is therefore also causing anxiety at the headquarters of the Danish Ministry of Foreign Affairs. What do diplomats fear? Possible Chinese punitive measures against Danish trade. China has previously used its economic muscle to punish countries that expand their cooperation with Taiwan. In addition, China does not always distinguish between state and civil society, so even a small private foundation meeting can make diplomats nervous.

The Alliance of Democracies Foundation is on China's blacklist—the sanctions list from 2021 along with a number of European Members of Parliament. This means a travel ban to China, but otherwise it has no practical effect on our work. The sanctions are a badge of honor—that our activities are being monitored by Beijing, where the regime is otherwise busy controlling 1.4 billion Chinese citizens.

The sanctioning of a democracy fund also illustrates how autocratic China, which likes to tell the world that China's foreign policy stands for non-interference in other countries' affairs, will nevertheless seek to decide what and especially who can speak on stage in Copenhagen thousands of kilometers from Beijing.

Therefore, I see the People's Republic of China very differently today than in 2005. In 2005, I visited Xiamen in Fujian Province at the invitation of the Chinese Ministry of Foreign Affairs among a group of European diplomats. From Xiamen, I could spot the island of Kinmen, which is part of Taiwan but just a short ferry ride away. I remember one of the Chinese diplomats telling me that the situation in the Taiwan Strait would be resolved peacefully through economic integration. In 2023, I stand on the other side—on the beach on Kinmen, looking across to the skyscrapers of Xiamen, China, where I can no longer enter. Now I doubt that peace will last.

Just as the outcome of the war in Ukraine will determine whether Europe can continue to call itself a continent based on the right of free people to choose their own form of government, the same is true for Taiwan in Asia.

IS TAIWAN'S RESILIENCE STRONG ENOUGH?

Will Taiwan become the next conflict zone after Ukraine? What have the Taiwanese learned from Ukraine's resistance struggle? What significance does a conflict over Taiwan have for us in Europe and globally? These are big questions and I seek answers to them.

So in late 2022 and early 2023, I traveled to Taiwan, where I met with Taiwanese politicians, businessmen and computer chip billionaires, military leaders, digital experts, Hong Kong and Chinese dissidents, and a pop singer whose songs are banned by China.

Those perspectives are my narrative of the battle for Taiwan. Here's how the rest of the book unfolds.

Chapter 2 explains Taiwan's complicated history sandwiched between China and the US, as well as key concepts such as the One China Policy.

Chapter 3 is about political resilience. Taiwan is politically deeply divided between the current ruling party, the Democratic Progressive Party (DPP) and the opposition Nationalist Party (KMT). The ruling party stands for an independent

Taiwanese identity and to prevent China from dominating Taiwan's politics. The Nationalist Party, which has its historical origins in China, stands for pragmatic cooperation and trade with China.

The relationship with China also divides the Taiwanese population. In Taiwanese election campaigns, DPP supporters view the KMT as traitors ready to "sell" Taiwan to China. KMT supporters see the DPP as a war party that instigates independence and lashes out too blindly at the US. In doing so, they believe the DPP is making Taiwan a military pawn—expendable—in the US-China power struggle.

In this fractured political landscape, there is ample opportunity for China to engage in various influence maneuvers. The Chinese dream is to use carrots and sticks to promote a Beijing-positive Taiwanese leader who voluntarily hands over the keys to Taiwan's independence and democracy to Beijing.

Chapter 4 is about how Ukraine's fight for freedom is also Taiwan's fight. At least that's how two young Taiwanese men, Jack and Tony, see it. During 2022, they have both fought in Ukraine on the frontline against the Russians. For Jack and Tony, Ukraine and Taiwan's freedom are connected. To them, it is not an abstract discussion. They feel it. They acted on that sentiment to prevent a world where the strong autocrat can rule over its smaller neighbor. My interviews with these young men made a big impression on me.

Chapter 5 is all about war. I sit down with military leaders and experts to unfold the different Chinese attack scenarios and how Taiwan can defend itself.

While I'm in Taiwan, President Tsai Ing-wen is increasing both the length of conscription and military budgets. The reason is clear: China's fighter jets make daily unwanted visits to the Taiwanese air defense zone. The threat can be heard. The president's move is intended to deter China militarily, so that Taiwan is perceived by China as a small but resilient hedgehog full of sharp defense spikes.

Ukraine is the little David defending itself against the Russian giant Goliath. In the same way, Taiwan is studying what it can learn from Ukraine—and from the battle of the small against the big.

But there are clear military differences between the two countries. Unlike Ukraine, Taiwan is an island. This makes it easier to defend against a large-scale invasion by sea. But it makes it harder to defend against military quarantines and blockades at sea, which can prove to be the most effective tool in China's military toolbox. In a quarantine or blockade situation at sea, it could prove difficult for the US and other democracies to assist Taiwan with food, medicine and military aid, as is the case in Ukraine today.

I visit the small Taiwanese islands that are in proximity to the Chinese mainland: another possible frontline. China could take inspiration from Russia, which began by invading Crimea in 2014, and China could seize a smaller island to test Taiwan—and the US.

Ultimately, all military scenarios hinge on the US's willingness to engage. A Chinese attack on Taiwan would likely bring the US into direct military conflict with China—two nuclear powers and the world's two largest navies and strongest militaries.

In Chapter 6, I'm attending a defense course with both the black bear warriors of Kuma Academy and the Florence Nightingale nurses of Forward Alliance. Taiwan's civil society is part of its strength and an important part of its resilience. Since the start of the Ukraine war, the influx of participants to such courses is massive. These civil society organizations run self-defense courses that train ordinary Taiwanese people in first aid, knowledge of Chinese weapon types and tools to identify Chinese disinformation online. The courses prepare the Taiwanese to cope as internally displaced people. Ukraine's refugees can seek safety in neighboring safe countries. In Taiwan's case, the sea is the only neighbor. The nearest Japanese island is over 100 km away in troubled waters.

Chapter 7 is all about computer chips. It's the hard currency of technological globalization. And Taiwan produces the bulk of the world's advanced chips. The epicenter is the city of Hsinchu, Taiwan's answer to Silicon Valley, which I visit. I speak with Robert Tsao and Wu Miin, two chip billionaires and leading pioneers in the industry. Without these chips, our technology-driven lives would grind to a halt. That's why experts label the chip industry Taiwan's "silicon shield", as silicon is the element that is the main component in a computer chip. Taiwan protects itself from an attack from China by playing such an essential role in world trade.

However, that shield is under erosion. Since 2022, the US is spending billions in government subsidies to develop chip production within its borders. Europe and Japan are doing the same. And Taiwan's leading computer chip company, TSMC, is being pressured to open factories in the US. At the same time, China is spending billions to catch up with the US and Taiwan.

The story of the chip industry is true geopolitics with several elements: the future of technological globalization, the US-China power struggle, billions of dollars, and Taiwan's economic and security survival.

In Chapter 8, I examine China's economic anaconda strategy towards Taiwan. Economically, dependence on China is hard to reduce accounting for about 40 percent of Taiwan's trade. The Tsai Ing-wen government sees trade with China as a security policy Achilles heel. The DPP government has actively tried to increase trade with other countries instead. But China is blocking Taiwan from entering into free trade agreements with other countries. Chinese pressure prevents this, citing the One China policy and economic threats. Overall, this means that Taiwan—even if the political system resists—is inevitably sucked towards China's large market, the world's second largest economy. Herein lies a great vulnerability for Taiwan. It might be China's strongest asset in the battle for Taiwan.

However, it's not just economic attraction. China is also using its economic muscle to put pressure on Taiwan, imposing bans on the import of certain Taiwanese goods. While I'm in Taiwan, the local beer, Taiwan Beer, is being put on Chinese ice.

Chapter 9 is about Taiwan's digital resilience against China's digital warfare. I get together with Audrey Tang, Taiwan's Minister of Digitalization and former hacker. She stands as a radical alternative to China's closedness and censorship. With her, all governance is open—our meeting and all other meetings are recorded and posted live online. No censorship. No need for citizens or journalists to ask for access to documents.

It is also with Tang that Taiwan's governmental response to China's disinformation is being molded. Transparency, education and an active civil society are key components. #FreetheFuture—set the future free—is the slogan and hashtag for Audrey Tang's ministry.

The free internet must be secured, and Tang is working to ensure constant internet connectivity so that China cannot black out Taiwan. This is a lesson learned from Ukraine, where free satellite accessing Elon Musk's Starlink company ensured that Russia could not black out Ukraine in the early stages of the war. Russia had succeeded with the digital blackout in Crimea during the 2014 invasion.

Taiwan relies on strategically important undersea cables for internet connectivity, but satellites are being launched and portable-sized 5G internet is being deployed to distribute the internet—to counter if China could cut the undersea cables to Taiwan. This is not science fiction. Mysteriously severed internet cables were experienced by the smaller Taiwanese archipelago of Matsu in the spring of 2023.

In Chapter 10, I write about Taiwan's role as an Asian bastion of free speech. It is now the only place in the Chinese-speaking world where it is possible to express your views without the threat of government repression. Chinese dissidents can also get their messages across in Taiwan. The people of Taiwan have fought hard for this freedom of expression against the authoritarian system that prevailed up until the 1990s.

The freedom to say what you want is also an additional reason why Xi Jinping wants to incorporate Taiwan and short-circuit their democratic system. Freedom is seen by Xi as a threat to his control society. This is in line with how Beijing has already cracked down on Hong Kong citizens' freedom of press and speech. Many from Hong Kong's democracy movement have since fled to Taiwan. I talk to them about their new life—in exile.

In chapter 11, I address the fateful years ahead. When and how can a conflict break out? I also share my thoughts on how we—also in Denmark and Europe—can do more to secure peace and help deter China from attacking Taiwan.

Europe's most powerful potential and contribution to ensuring continued peace is in the economic sphere. Together in the EU, we should use the threat of trade sanctions to keep

China from attacking Taiwan. Should we be forced to implement such sanctions, it will be costly for European companies, workers and consumers, but we must not forget that at stake are the fundamental values, which our societies are built on.

When I started this book project and went to Taiwan, a friend wrote to me asking why I bothered. "They're all Chinese and have to figure it out for themselves. We shouldn't interfere with that."

Another friend cynically joked over a drink that it was a good thing I was rushing out there, as it would probably be my last visit to Taiwan before it is taken over by China.

I hope that the first friend and other like-minded readers will join me on my journey into the struggle for Taiwan's democracy and understand—as I have realized—why Taiwan's freedom and democracy is not only vital to the 23 million citizens, but to all of us freedom-minded people, and especially significant in the global power struggle with—and against—China's authoritarian model.

In response to the other friend, I sincerely hope that none of us will see a world where China successfully takes over Taiwan and denies its citizens their freedom. That would be a much less free world.

CHAPTER 2

Taiwan and the Republic of China's complicated history with China and the US—and the rest of the world

What is Taiwan? Is it even a country? The answer depends on who you ask.

It demands a quick tour of history to understand the background. The basic concepts are the difference between the People's Republic of China—what we colloquially call China—and the Republic of China, which we refer to as Taiwan. Inextricably linked to the history of the People's Republic of China and the Republic of China/Taiwan are the historical leaders Sun Yat-sen, Mao Zedong and Chiang Kai-shek in key roles.

At the end of the red carpet in the lobby in the Ministry of Foreign Affairs in Taipei, I'm greeted by a large emblem with the Republic of China. And when I enter the main staircase inside the Presidential Building in Taipei, a large bust of Sun Yat-sen, the founder of the Republic of China in 1912, looks at me.

Similarly, a large painting of Sun Yat-sen presides in the main hall of the parliament. For proponents of a distinct

Taiwanese identity, the affinity with the Republic of China and Sun Yat-sen makes little sense today. When I visit the parliament, Freddy Lim, a Taiwanese independent parliamentarian and rock musician, tells me that he would like to see Sun's portrait taken down. Sun is mainly associated with China's history and Sun only visited Taiwan a few times. Lim jokes that I've been in Taiwan longer than Sun.

China and Taiwan relations are also linked to the much discussed one-China policy and what it means from the perspective of Beijing (where it is referred to as the one-China principle), Washington and Brussels, and why Taiwan—a democratic society—is such a squeezed entity in the international community.

TAIWAN'S HISTORY—IN BRIEF

The landmark year is 1949. After World War IIs ending in 1945, the Chinese civil war between the Nationalists—led by Chiang Kai-shek—and the Communists—led by Mao Zedong—continued for four years. In 1949, the communists gain the upper hand. In Beijing in front of the Forbidden City, the old residence of the emperors, the communist leader Mao proclaims the People's Republic of China on October 1, 1949. Chiang Kai-shek and his forces retreat.

Chiang therefore also relocates his army to the island of Taiwan, which had been a colony and occupied by Japan from 1895 until the end of World War II. As part of the Second World War peace negotiations, Taiwan was handed over to the Republic of China at the request of Chiang Kai-shek's government. Interestingly, many Communist Party supporters today refer to these negotiations, conducted by the archenemy during the civil war, when arguing for China's historic right to Taiwan.

Chiang brings with him to Taiwan the Republic of China, which was established in 1912 by Sun Yat-sen, the successor to the last emperor. The Republic endures in Taiwan to this day. In Communist China, Sun Yat-sen is also recognized as an important historical figure who ended the empire. Chiang Kai-shek also brings a large army with him and over a million people move with him—all of Chinese origin. That event ties Taiwan to Chinese history.

Further back in history, Taiwan is referred to as "Ilha Formosa", the beautiful island. This name was suggested by a Portuguese explorer in the 1540s. However, it was Spain and the Netherlands who held colonial settlements on southern and northern Taiwan respectively throughout the 17th century. At the same time, mainland Chinese settlers continuously moved to the island. A colorful pirate named Koxinga and his descendants ruled Taiwan independently for a period from 1661 to 1683.

That year, Taiwan was incorporated into the Ching Empire. The island briefly became a province of China along with Fujian, the Chinese province bordering the Taiwan Strait. This is where many Taiwanese have their family roots. Today, however, there is much debate among Taiwanese as to how much influence the Ching Empire had on Taiwan. Regardless, Taiwan remained a loose part of Ching Dynasty China until 1895, when Japan took over the island as part of the peace settlement after the Sino-Japanese War.

That also explains why Taiwan plays such an important role in Chinese historical nationalism in the Communist Party today. Since the 1990s, nationalism has replaced Marx and Engels in Chinese school textbooks. The Taiwan question is viewed as part of the confrontation with Japan specifically and more generally with the 19th century's historical injustices against China in the form of colonization by a number of Western powers as well. The period is referred to as the "100 years of humiliation". Only a strong China led by Xi Jinping and the Communist Party can insure against similar defeats, is the conclusion of this narrative of China's history. Therefore, the year 2049 plays a key role for Communist China, which by the time it celebrates its 100th birthday aims to be a global superpower with Taiwan as part of China.

But what is left out of Chinese school textbooks and official history propaganda is that the Communist Party and the People's Republic of China have never had control over Taiwan. The red flag with the yellow stars has never flown over Taiwan. China's school textbooks also omit about Taiwan's current system, where its citizens vote in free elections and enjoy freedom of speech.

In 1895, during the peace negotiations between Ching's China and Japan, the Taiwanese took the initiative when they heard about the planned handover to Japan. They established the Republic of Formosa, one of the first republics in Asia. However, that republic was short-lived.

It took less than five months for Japanese troops to storm Taiwan and the island was transformed into a Japanese colony. Japan's rule was brutal and heavy-handed in some areas, but it was a period of economic prosperity and to this day there is a close connection between Taiwan and Japan. Many Taiwanese still feel closely connected to Japan and its culture. Judging by the number of Japanese tourists and political statements, the feeling is mutual. It is said that the best Japanese food outside of Japan is found in Taiwan.

Taiwan is home to an indigenous population that has inhabited the island for thousands of years. They were there before Western colonial powers, before the Chinese and before the Japanese. They have similarities with inhabitants of Southeast Asia and other Polynesian and Melanesian Pacific islands. Jonathan Tseng, a Taiwanese soldier who fought in Ukraine in 2022 and who I write about in chapter 4, is from the Amis people living on the east coast of Taiwan.

For these people, who today make up around two percent of the population, the past centuries have been one long history of colonization under different masters. Still, the current democratic system in Taiwan has given them better opportunities for participation and social equality than before.

THE HARD ROAD FROM CHIANG KAI-SHEK TO DEMOCRACY

When I ask ordinary people in Taiwan about their country, the answer is that they are Taiwanese and citizens of their own country. They have it all, just like we do in Denmark. The Republic of China/Taiwan functions as a sovereign state with its own banknotes, passports, military, police and democratically elected politicians and well-founded freedoms.

In terms of freedoms, things were not looking good in 1949. Chiang Kai-shek was an autocratic leader like Mao. His regime enforced the longest martial law in world history at the time—38 years of heavy repression of dissidents and of any possibility of living out Taiwanese identity. The Taiwanese language was banned, only Mandarin Chinese was allowed.

"Chiang was a dictator," explains Emily Wu, a Taiwanese journalist in her thirties and founder of the independent media outlet Ghost Island Media, as we visit the Chiang Kai-shek memorial in central Taipei. We have to climb many steps to reach Chiang, who sits at the top of a white Chinese temple. Chiang sits in a chair and looks out over the city, just like Lincoln does at his Washington DC memorial. The monument is, of course, controversial in today's Taiwan, and some Taiwanese want it removed.

When Emily Wu was a child, Chiang's statues were everywhere in Taiwan—including her school. Today, most of the statues have been taken down, but near Taipei there is a Chiang statue cemetery where they are stored.

After Chiang's death in 1975 and a long transition period with his son Chiang Ching-kuo in power, a democratization process set in that led to the first free presidential election in 1996.

But the process was harsh. During Chiang Kai-shek's so-called White Terror, especially in the 1950s, civilians were executed on a large scale. Thousands were sent to re-education camps. The official intention was to root out communist spies, but the regime went much broader, targeting voices critical of the government, supporters of an independent Taiwanese identity.

Today, tourists can take idyllic snorkeling trips to Green Island, a small island gem off the east coast of Taiwan. Under Chiang, the island was used as a re-education camp. While I'm in Taiwan, the movie "Untold herstory" is released, which tells the heartbreaking story of the unity among a group of female prisoners on the island in the 1950s. The Chiang Kai-shek period continues to trace its dark historical footprint to modern-day Taiwan, but the movie is one way to reckon with this painful history. This is possible now in a free society.

Since 1996, Taiwan has held frequent democratic elections. The last presidential election took place in 2020, when Tsai

Ing-wen of the Democratic Progressive Party was re-elected president. The party, abbreviated DPP, stands for an autonomous Taiwanese identity and an independence-seeking approach to mainland China. Democratization has also meant Taiwanization. The party was illegal until democratization began and was first allowed to run in 1992 for the parliamentary election and in 1996 for the presidential election.

On the other side of the political spectrum is the Guomindang; the Nationalist Party that emigrated with Chiang Kai-shek from the mainland. Although the Nationalists fought against the communists in the civil war of the 1940s, they have strong ties to China, where most have family origins. The Nationalist Party is more in tune with the Communists in Beijing that there should be only one China on the world stage, but they disagree on who is its rightful leader. It goes back to who won—or should have won—the civil war in the 1940s.

ONE CHINA POLICY AND THE CHOICE
BETWEEN PRC AND ROC

For many decades, the People's Republic of China (PRC) and the Republic of China (ROC) fought to be internationally recognized as "the one and only China". Both sides agreed that there was only one China. But from there, it was an either-or decision for third countries. Which China to choose—the Republic or the People's Republic of China? In 1949, the diplomatic map looked very different from today—and more favorable to the Republic of China. In the founding year, only other communist countries recognized the People's Republic of China and Mao's communist rule. The People's Republic of China was not present in the United Nations until 1971, nor in the UN Security Council. There sat the Republic of China, ruled from Taiwan by Chiang Kai-shek.

Today, the People's Republic of China has won the international game of recognition. The Republic of China is off the UN list of countries since 1971. Neither can one find Taiwan. Most countries recognize Beijing and pursue some form of one-China policy. Beijing refers to it even more broadly as a one-China principle; almost in line with international ground rules in the UN. In their view, the one-China principle means that other countries accept that Taiwan is an inseparable part of China, and that Beijing has the right to use all means, including violence and military force.

The endgame for the Republic of China is on display in the lobby of the Ministry of Foreign Affairs in Taipei. Here are the flags displayed of the countries that still recognize the Republic of China. Rather unfamiliar flags—even to me as a former diplomat. The flags belong to idyllic but little-known Pacific islands and somewhat larger Latin American countries such as Guatemala, Belize and Paraguay. By March 2023, only 13 flags remain, as Honduras switched recognition from Taipei to Beijing.

People all over the world who talk about or have contacts with Taiwan can be subjected to pressure from China. In Denmark, we experienced that with the arrival of the Chinese pandas at Frederiksberg Zoological Garden in 2019. China's diplomats inspected the display in the zoo. They were dissatisfied with the map, which showed Taiwan in a different color than the rest of China. After consultation with the Danish Ministry of Foreign Affairs, the Zoo revised the map. The solution was: Taiwan disappeared. As the then head of the zoo, Bengt Holst, said to the Berlingske, a Danish media outlet: "To avoid that debate, we made a new map zoomed in on the three provinces in China with pandas." The action can be seen as innocent diplomacy, ensuring Chinese goodwill and that the pandas remain in Copenhagen, but can also be seen as a bow to China's dictates regarding Taiwan, which Western democracies are increasingly accepting on home ground. That's how I see it.

The lack of international recognition of Taiwan in the UN and its sub-organizations also leads to ridiculous situations that endanger global health. China prevents the World Health Organization (WHO) from cooperating with Taiwan's health authorities. Yet Taiwan's health authorities were the first to sound the alarm over the COVID-19 outbreak in China. The Taiwanese authorities initiated health screenings of air travelers from Wuhan as early as December 2019. Their warning and preparedness could have helped the rest of the world better navigate the COVID-19 pandemic, where in the early months, China simply kept international flights open, allowing the disease to spread globally.

US AND BIDEN'S TAIWAN POLICY—STRATEGIC AMBIGUITY AND CLARITY

If we look around the globe and ask about Taiwan's role in Washington, we get an "it's complicated" answer. Until 1979, the US recognized the Republic of China, i.e. the government in Taiwan, as the legal international representative. The US also had a bilateral defense treaty with the Republic of China led by Chiang Kai-shek, who, despite his authoritarian leadership style, was seen as part of the bulwark against the communists in China and the Soviet Union. Until 1971, the Republic of China also held China's seat in the UN, including veto power in the powerful Security Council.

In 1979, US President Jimmy Carter switched diplomatic recognition from Taipei to Beijing. It was part of a process set in motion by the previous Republican President Richard Nixon's historic 1972 visit to Beijing and meeting with Mao. Nixon's intention was to weaken the Soviet Union by the US conducting pragmatic cooperation with Communist China, which under Mao had also distanced itself from Moscow.

In response, the US Congress, unhappy with the tough way the US government had treated the now former ally, passed legislation named the Taiwan Relations Act in 1979. The act stipulates that the US must help Taiwan, including by selling military equipment to Taiwan. Prior to this, the US had abrogated the treaty-based agreement to defend Taiwan.

Current US policy towards Taiwan is often referred to as "strategic ambiguity", although it is not an official label. It means that the US is not obliged to automatically come to Taiwan's aid in the event of an attack, but it does not rule it out either. President Biden has provided his version of the policy by repeatedly stating that he will defend Taiwan militarily.

The US pursues its own one-China policy, not the version dictated by the Communist Party from Beijing. The US recognizes that China sees Taiwan as part of China, but the US itself regards Taiwan's status as an unresolved issue. In addition, US policy is to maintain the status quo in the Taiwan Strait. There is a good bit of diplomatic ambiguity built into this, hence the label.

However, if China attacked and took Taiwan without the US reacting, there is no doubt that US credibility in Asia in general, and in particular with Asian allies such as Japan and South Korea, would suffer lasting damage. It is likely that very soon after such a development, South Korea and probably also Japan would produce their own nuclear weapons to secure themselves in the shifting military balance of power with China. Taiwan's key role for the US and globally in the production of electronic chips would also make it impossible for the US to accept China taking over the island and its chip production.

In recent years, the US relationship with Taiwan has become closer. President Donald Trump spoke with Taiwanese President Tsai Ing-wen just after he was elected in November 2016. The Trump administration also increased military sales to Taiwan. However, Trump personally took a more trade-oriented approach to Taiwan. According to sources in his administration, Trump was willing to "sell" Taiwan to China for a better trade deal for the US.

The increased focus on Taiwan is also seen both in Congress and in the two parties, Democrats and Republicans. Nancy Pelosi, the former leader of the House of Representatives, visited Taiwan in August 2022. Her plane was the most followed ever on flight-tracking apps, with millions of followers around the world. Chinese bloggers and nationalists on the mainland even went so far as to call for the Chinese Air Force to shoot down the plane. Fortunately, that didn't happen. Instead, in the days that followed, China's military conducted their largest-ever military exercises around Taiwan with planes, navy and missiles.

Pelosi's Republican successor as leader of the House of Representatives, Kevin McCarthy, met with President Tsai Ing-wen in April 2023, triggering another round of Chinese military exercises around Taiwan. Among Republicans, there are now many elected officials who want to break from the official policy of strategic ambiguity and shift to "strategic clarity". That is, some form of increased recognition of Taiwan and the US security commitment to defend the island nation.

When I'm in Taiwan in November 2022, I meet with Will Hurd, former member of Congress from Texas and presidential candidate in the Republican primaries in 2023. Over a nice dumpling dinner, Will argues that the US must shift its position to strategic clarity. It is politically the only viable option, he says, if you want to convince the American public that the fight for Taiwan's democracy is worth fighting for the US. That must be spelled out—without diplomatic one-China-twists. Otherwise, the average American won't understand why it's also their fight for freedom. Or why American soldiers may need to fight for Taiwan at some point.

Joe Biden has also tinkered with the strategic ambiguity several times by stating that he will defend Taiwan militarily if China attacks the island state. And Biden is so old in the game—and in American politics—that as a young senator he voted for the Taiwan Relations Act in 1979. This means that Biden is familiar with American politics, but also that his personal position is clearly to defend Taiwan.

Joe Biden refers to our era as divided between democracies and autocracies. In Asia, the dividing line between the two forms of government runs right across the Taiwan Strait. On the one side, the authoritarian People's Republic led by communist leader Xi Jinping, which has become increasingly authoritarian. On the other, democratic Taiwan, which continues to rise in international democracy polls. Freedom versus surveillance. Democracy versus top-down control. It's night and day.

When Biden met with Xi Jinping at the G-20 summit in Bali in November 2022, Taiwan was also a major point of discussion. The US and Chinese press releases after the meeting illustrated the stark discrepancy. Xi said that "the Taiwan issue is the core of core interests" for China and that there is a red line that must not be crossed by the US in supporting Taiwanese independence. Biden, on the other hand, emphasized China's "aggressive actions against Taiwan, which…can jeopardize global prosperity". When the two presidents met in San Francisco in November 2023, Biden added possible Chinese election interference in Taiwan's January 2024 presidential elections to the list of concerns.

THE EU AND DENMARK'S ONE-CHINA POLICY

If you ask about Taiwan's status in Europe or more locally in Copenhagen, the answer is that Denmark has a one-China policy, which means that it only recognizes the People's Republic of China.

Unlike the United States, Denmark never recognized the Republic of China when it moved to Taiwan in 1949. Denmark established diplomatic relations directly with the People's Republic of China in 1950. It was one of the first Western countries to do so after Mao proclaimed the birth of the new China in Tiananmen Square in October 1949.

However, within the framework of the one-China policy, there is also some room for ambiguity and maneuver about Taiwan and its status. Denmark and the EU regularly call for maintaining the status quo in the Taiwan Strait and for the parties to behave peacefully, such as when China rained missiles into the sea after Pelosi's visit to Taiwan in August 2022.

French President Emmanuel Macron sparked a renewed debate on the EU's Taiwan policy when, during his visit to China in April 2023, he called for European neutrality on the issue. German Foreign Minister Annalena Baerbock traveled to Beijing a few days later and gave her version: a clear warning to China to stay out of Taiwan militarily.

That warning was given with good reason. While I was in Taiwan, there were almost daily encounters in the Taiwan Air Defense Zone between China's fighter jets and the Taiwanese Air Force. The Chinese Air Force is trying to normalize their presence to such an extent that the Taiwanese and the outside world don't know when the drills turn serious. It's the story of "cry wolf" in a dangerous Chinese version.

BEIJING'S ONE CHINA PRINCIPLE AND TAIWAN'S "REUNIFICATION"

If you ask about Taiwan's status in Beijing, the answer is quite simple. Taiwan is a province that is part of the People's Republic of China and, in practical terms, must be "reunited" with the People's Republic of China as soon as possible. It's solely a question of when and how. Preferably peacefully—but otherwise, China's regime has other methods, including military solutions.

After a takeover, Taiwan's citizens will have to be "re-educated" to fit in with the People's Republic of China, as the Chinese ambassador to France, Lu Shaye, scarily outlined on the BFMTV news program in August 2022. This points to a grim fate, as harsh as that of Hong Kong, whose freedoms disappeared with the introduction of the Chinese National Security Law in 2020. It also points to a future as brainwashed as that of the Uighurs in Xinjiang, who are being subjected to a massive re-education project.

From the perspective of the Communist Party, the Taiwan question is about historical justice. It is about the unfinished civil war itself, where the communists were suppressed and almost completely wiped out but ended up winning the entire mainland. Only one last rebel bastion remains: Taiwan.

In terms of military strategy, Taiwan plays a key maritime role as an outpost in the island chain protected by the US and its Asian allies: Japan, the Philippines and South Korea. There is little doubt that Taiwan is also a great listening station for the Americans close to the mainland. From China's perspective, Taiwan is also militarily significant for maritime control and access to the Pacific Ocean.

In 1995–96, President Bill Clinton moved US aircraft carriers into the Taiwan Strait, putting an end to Chinese military action against Taiwan. In April 2023, China deployed its aircraft carrier Shandong past the eastern shores of Taiwan to demonstrate its ability to conduct a maritime encirclement of Taiwan. The balance of power is shifting in these years.

So far, however, the peace has held. Everyone knows their place in the game, is the classic analysis that I was brought up with as a Danish diplomat. Everyone will lose from a war. That's why it won't happen. But Russia's invasion of Ukraine shows that the calculus can be different for despots. Whether it's Putin or Xi.

China is currently going through an economic tough transition after COVID-19. The Communist Party and Xi no longer automatically deliver economic prosperity. That was the long-standing authoritarian contract with the Chinese people: We—the Communist Party—deliver prosperity. You—the 1.4 billion people—keep quiet and refrain from criticizing the party. That contract is broken with slow growth and high youth unemployment. Now other rallying points are needed. This may give Xi the desire for military adventures to rally the Chinese people around the nation—and him. In addition, Xi Jinping must show results in 2027 when his Secretary General post is up for renewal for another five-year term.

Historically, Taiwan's status is fundamentally contested and part of the great power game between the world's number one and two, the United States and the People's Republic of China. But there is no doubt about what Taiwan is to its citizens: their democratic homeland.

CHAPTER 3

Taiwan's political resilience—who secures the peace?

"Taiwan's political life is about unresolved identity," a Taiwanese political campaign operative explains to me. That line frames the situation accurately.

Polls from 2022 show that 60 percent of the Taiwanese population identify as Taiwanese. 33 percent see themselves as both Taiwanese and Chinese. Only around two percent see themselves as exclusively Chinese. That figure was as high as 25 percent in 1992, when Taiwan embarked on its first free parliamentary elections.

Democratization has resulted in a stronger Taiwanese identity. This is the voter base that the DPP represents. The Nationalist Party, whose voter base came from the mainland with Chiang Kai-shek's army in 1949, stands for stronger ties to China. Some KMT supporters, among the older generation, continue to feel strong ties with mainland China.

On the extremes of Taiwanese politics are five percent who want independence here and now, and just over one percent—the lowest ever in 2022—who want unification with China right here and now. In this sense, Taiwanese politics is polarized. When tempers flare as during election campaigns, die-hard DPP voters perceive their KMT opponents as being in cahoots with China to "sell" Taiwan. Conversely, KMT voters see the DPP's moves towards Taiwanese independence and increased cooperation with the US as irresponsible because their actions could spark China to start a war.

On April 7, 2023, two presidents land in Taipei from separate trips abroad, illustrating the divisions.

President Tsai Ing-wen went to the United States. During her trip, she met with the then Speaker of the House of Representatives, Kevin McCarthy, and a number of other members of Congress at the Reagan Library in Los Angeles. Tsai said that with the support of the US, Taiwanese people do not feel alone or isolated. Her policy is to forge closer ties with the US to secure Taiwan.

Her predecessor, President Ma Ying-jeou, returned from China. He is the first President since the civil war in 1949 to undertake such a trip. There is a personal element for the 72-year-old ex-president, visiting his grandparents' burial site in Hunan province. But Ma also carries a political message. During a presentation to Chinese students in Changsha, he states that Taiwan and China are part of one China. The statement has some ambiguity, as Ma refers to the Republic of China as his one China. But overall, the contrast between the two presidents' journeys couldn't be greater: US or China.

Taiwan's politics are therefore existential for the country. Which politicians do Taiwanese voters trust to keep the peace with China? It's about the survival of the island and each citizen. Above 50 percent of voters want to maintain the current status quo and peace. The desire for continued peace unites voters from both parties. In a sense, this is the center of Taiwanese politics.

TSAI ING-WEN—FROM CAT LADY TO CAT WARRIOR

The cat is wearing a nice pair of bunny ears. A smiling lady with black hair and glasses holds up the cat. This is to mark the Lunar New Year and the beginning of the Year of the Rabbit at the end of January 2023. The post receives thousands of positive comments on Instagram. It is President Tsai Ing-wen with one of her cats. In the caption, she adds motherly and admonishing words to her followers to dress properly and drive safely in traffic for the Lunar New Year.

Cats are also popular in Taiwanese politics. Tsai Ing-wen likes to play the role of the nation's cat lady leader. She was elected president in 2016 as the first woman in Taiwan's history and re-elected in 2020, when China's repression of Hong Kong helped her secure a solid election victory because her opponent from the Nationalist Party was deemed too China-friendly by voters. She is progressive and has enabled the legalization of same sex marriage: the first country in Asia. And with her, other women have also broken through the political glass ceiling, increasing the number of women in parliament to over 40 percent during her tenure.

Tsai Ing-wen represents the Democratic Progressive Party (DPP), which can be compared to the German Green Party. Tsai has set high climate goals and also decided to phase out nuclear power. Because of China's military threats, she is increasingly taking a more combative role as the nation's commander-in-chief.

The Ukraine war has intensified her focus on Taiwan's defense. When she addresses the nation's armed forces, she wears a green camouflage helmet and bulletproof vest in camouflage colors. She resembles President Volodymyr Zelenskyy in her simple army outfit.

I met President Tsai together with Anders Fogh Rasmussen on a Wednesday in early January 2023 in the Red Presidential Building, centrally located in Taipei. The building is a long-standing center of power, already during the colonial era with Japanese governors and for years during the authoritarian leader Chiang Kai-shek.

We are escorted into a classic meeting room with calligraphy on the wall, deep armchairs that you almost disappear into and an aesthetic arrangement of pink orchids in the background. On the way up the stairs, we pass a bust of Sun Yat-sen, the founder of the Republic of China. It is Chinese in style. The set up reminds me of similar official meeting rooms in China. It reflects the ambiguity of Tsai being elected President of the Republic of China, even though she and her party speaks about their country as Taiwan and advocate for an independent Taiwanese identity.

Tsai enters the room wearing a blue-gray suit with black pants and flat shoes. Neat and practical, just like Merkel, whom Tsai has also cited as an inspiration. Tsai is in her mid-sixties but looks younger.

Tsai explains to us that "the Taiwanese have lived under an autocratic system. They know they cannot take their current freedom for granted". China is the external authoritarian threat. Therefore, as leader of Taiwan, Tsai has worked to increase Taiwan's resilience against China. Economically, she has worked to ensure Taiwan has other options than being dependent on the Chinese market. I write about this in Chapter 8. Militarily, she has increased the defense budget and—while I am in Taiwan—launched an extension of military conscription from 4 to 12 months.

Digitally, Tsai's government has taken action against Chinese disinformation, which I discuss in depth with Minister of Digitalization Audrey Tang in Chapter 9. Tsai mentions to us her particular concern about the rise of the Chinese app TikTok. Her government has already banned TikTok on public work phones by 2022. Denmark and other European countries later followed suit.

Diplomatically, she has strengthened cooperation with the US and Europe. She perceives her public speeches at the Copenhagen Democracy Summit as part of her efforts to place Taiwan on the world map of democratic countries.

She summarizes her approach as follows: "Taiwan's story is about resilience." The main objective is to deter China from attacking Taiwan. This is the legacy she would like to leave behind when she leaves office in May 2024. A former presidential aide sums up her stance to the New York Times: "She wants to push Taiwan's position as an independent country as far as she can without the Americans losing trust in her."

The Ukraine war has a direct effect on Taiwan, Tsai explains that "China is closely following what is happening in Ukraine. If democratic countries get tired of supporting Ukraine, it will encourage Xi Jinping." Therefore, according to Tsai, the outcome of the war in Ukraine is pivotal for the Taiwan Strait and for the conclusions Xi Jinping draws from it.

When Tsai lays out her policies, she is measured and precise. Every word is weighed carefully. Earlier in her career, she was a university law professor. Her field of work was international trade negotiations, including Taiwan's accession to the World Trade Organization (WTO) in 2002.

Under former DPP President Chen Shui-bian from 2000 to 2008, she held several key positions until she became party chairman in 2008. She saw from the inside how Chen's proposal for a referendum on Taiwan's admission to the UN was opposed by China—predictably—but also by the US. President

Bush's administration—with Iraq and the Middle East as its main priorities—expressed concern about the referendum, much to Beijing's delight. Secretary of State Condoleezza Rice called the move "provocative". At the time, the US indicated that Taiwan could not count on US assistance if its government took a destabilizing action that would ignite Beijing.

I think Tsai took a lesson from the referendum process not to alienate the US and thereby undermine support for Taiwan by provoking China. Tsai emphasizes that "China is looking for an excuse in Taiwanese politics to react".

We hear a similar message from Vice President Lai Ching-te, who is the presidential candidate for the DPP in the 2024 election. "I'm not trying to provoke," he emphasizes. Lai knows that China is painting a propaganda picture of him as a dangerous separatist using that narrative to justify a reaction preceding the elections on 13 January 2024.

It's up to DPP leaders to strike a balance that keeps China at bay, US support steady and Taiwanese voters satisfied.

China has cut off official contacts with Tsai during her tenure because she represents the DPP, which is seen in Beijing as separatist and does not accept the one-China policy. Nevertheless, Tsai emphasizes her willingness to engage with China, again reflecting her balanced approach. As she concludes: "We don't provoke, but we don't bow down either." With her gradually tougher image, Tsai is also referred to in the press as the "cat warrior".

FIGHTING SPIRIT AND BOXING GLOVES FROM UKRAINE

I am welcomed with fighting spirit by Foreign Minister Joseph Wu. He has been in that position since 2018, and prior to that, he worked for President Tsai in the National Security Council.

We meet at the Taiwanese Ministry of Foreign Affairs to talk about the Tsai administration's response to the Ukraine war and what Taiwan can learn from Ukraine's defense.

"These are Klitschko's boxing gloves," explains a proud Joseph Wu. He points to a pair of giant autographed boxing gloves hosted in a glass display. The gloves are from the mayor of Kyiv, Vitali Klitschko, who has a past as a heavyweight boxer. Wu received the gloves as a thanks for Taiwan's support to Kyiv's citizens with emergency aid and electric generators.

On Twitter in November 2022, Joseph Wu posted a photo of himself in a fighting stance with the gloves on. "We box against authoritarianism" the caption reads. He is standing in front of a Ukrainian flag with autographs from the front. A flag he received as a gift from grateful Ukrainians. He clearly sees a parallel in the Ukrainians' struggle against an aggressive authoritarian neighbor.

In practice, solidarity between the countries is a little more complicated, as Ukraine, like most other countries, abides by a one-China policy and therefore has no diplomatic relations with Taiwan. In practice, this means that Joseph Wu can't just pick up the phone and call his Ukrainian foreign minister colleague. Therefore, from the beginning of the war, Taiwanese donations to Ukraine have passed through Ukrainian cities and their mayors, civil society organizations or parliamentarians, or even through the Orthodox Church, whose leadership Wu had a video call with in June 2022.

Joseph Wu recalls February 24, 2022 as a terrible day. The reports and images from the war hit not only the Taiwanese government, but the entire Taiwanese people hard, even though Ukraine is thousands of kilometers away, and even though there was limited knowledge of the country before the war.

Wu explains why: the Taiwanese witnessed a democracy being attacked by an authoritarian regime without any provocation. The feeling in Taiwan was: "It could be us." Therefore, the instinctive reaction from the Taiwanese government was: "How can we best help Ukraine?" and "How do we secure ourselves against something similar?".

When the Ukrainian government called for the international community to support the country, the Taiwanese government rushed to contribute. In just one week, 27 tons of medicine was collected and sent to Ukraine. Wu mentions that Taiwan received assistance with the delivery from Poland because Taiwan does not have a representative office in Ukraine.

Ordinary Taiwanese citizens also wanted to contribute. Following popular demand, the Ministry of Foreign Affairs set up a bank account for transfers, and within a month, the equivalent of about 33 million US dollars was transferred to assist Ukrainian refugees.

The Taiwanese also wanted to contribute goods such as milk powder to Ukraine's population, so the Ministry of Foreign Affairs spontaneously opened their cellar garage. They were expecting around 10–20 tons. Instead, over 600 tons of goods were quickly delivered. Wu mentions that the amount of charity was touching for the employees of the Ministry of Foreign Affairs, but also overwhelming. Taiwanese civil society organizations stepped in to help organize and pack so that the Ministry of Foreign Affairs didn't drown in milk powder and blankets.

We turn to the question of what lessons the Taiwanese government is learning from the Ukraine war.

"The first lesson is the determination. We saw the Ukrainians fighting for the country, it's truly inspirational. They are very brave", Wu says. He sees in his own population an increased willingness to defend Taiwan.

The second point is "the best possible asymmetric strategy"—a military term for a David versus Goliath approach. How can Taiwan, as a small country, defend itself against China with a much larger military? The whole society must be mobilized around the defense effort. There is much to learn from Ukraine, which has held firm against the much larger Russian army.

The third lesson is the importance of solid international support. Ukraine has received military, economic and humanitarian support. Taiwan would need the same support if China attacks. Wu is a realist. He knows that the one-China policy makes international solidarity with Taiwan harder than for Ukraine, which is recognized in the UN, but Wu is encouraged by the many foreign parliamentarians who visit Taiwan to show support.

There is almost a tidal wave of visits during the months I am in Taiwan. They come from the US Congress, the European Parliament, the German, South Korean, Polish and Spanish parliaments. In May 2023, I speak to former British Prime Minister Liz Truss—now a Member of Parliament—before she heads of to visit Taiwan to show her support. But there is still a long way to go from a parliamentary support visit to European countries providing military equipment to Taiwan. In that regard, the fear of Chinese retaliation is too big. Currently, only the United States supplies arms to Taiwan.

Wu emphasizes another key difference between Taiwan and Ukraine: the water surrounding Taiwan. A Chinese naval quarantine or blockade worries Wu. In such a situation, Taiwan could run out of both energy and ammunition. Only the active military involvement of the US would secure Taiwan's maritime supply chains.

Finally, there is political resilience. Can Taiwan's political parties unite in a confrontation with China? The current ruling party, the DPP, sees itself as the spearhead of democracy in Taiwan. As presidential front-runner and Vice President Lai Ching-te explains, the DPP first fought against the authoritarian Nationalist Party, KMT, and now against China's authoritarian pressures.

Several DPP politicians emphasize to me that China's dream situation is to elect a compliant leader in Taiwan who voluntarily submits to Beijing. That way, China could win the battle for Taiwan's democracy without firing a bullet. In the DPP's reading, it was a close call under KMT President Ma Ying-jeou, who was close with China and even met with Xi Jinping in 2015 in Singapore.

THE NATIONALIST PARTY, KMT, WITH A PENCHANT FOR THE—REPUBLIC OF—CHINA

To hear from the other side of Taiwan's political spectrum, I met with the KMT's international department and, together with Anders Fogh Rasmussen, with the party's Secretary General Eric Chu.

Eric is an accomplished politician who lost the presidential election to Tsai Ing-wen in 2016, but beat her one round earlier in the 2012 Taipei mayoral election. Eric no longer commands sufficient support for another run for president. KMT's presidential candidate for January 2024 is New Taipei Mayor Hou You-yi flanked by vice-presidential candidate Jaw Shau-kong. But Eric Chu continues to play a leading role in setting policy for the KMT.

We are welcomed into a meeting room at the party headquarters, where Eric sits in front of a large painting of Sun Yat-sen, the man who founded the Nationalist Party in the 1890s and later the Republic of China. The Nationalist Party is Asia's oldest democratic party, Eric Chu points out to us.

Eric rejects the notion that the KMT can be described as pro-Chinese. The KMT is the party in Taiwan that has fought against the communists on the mainland—albeit back during the Cold War, he emphasizes.

Eric is a pragmatist. After several elections—even lost ones—he knows that Taiwan's middle-of-the-road voters want the status quo. In the last presidential election in 2020, the KMT lost badly with candidate Han Kuo-yu receiving less than 40% of the vote. Voters saw him as too pro-Chinese and unresponsive to China's crackdown on Hong Kong, which dominated the election agenda.

On the other hand, KMT took revenge in the local elections on November 26, 2022, where I was an election observer in Taipei. KMT candidates swept in everywhere—including the important mayoral seats. Taipei in particular attracted attention, with Chiang Wan-an taking the post. Such a stinging defeat that President Tsai Ing-wen resigned as DPP party leader after the election.

KMT is fine with the official name "Republic of China". "It's our country," as Eric explains. In that sense, it has been an independent country since 1912, the year the empire fell in

China and the republic was proclaimed. Therefore, the KMT does not want to pursue further independence under the name Taiwan. This is a clear difference from the DPP, whose voters demand greater recognition as Taiwan.

Basically, KMT identifies itself with the Republic of China and with Chinese civilization. During the visit to the KMT headquarters, I ponder how the KMT flag and the national flag are quite identical with white stars. It shows Taiwan's past as a one-party system under Chiang Kai-shek and emphasizes the symbiosis that used to exist between the Republic of China and the Nationalist Party.

I notice, however, that when Eric Chu talks about the history of the KMT, he deftly avoids mentioning Chiang Kai-shek. Eric is well aware that, apart from some nostalgic KMT voters, Chiang is perceived by a large part of the population—and by foreign visitors like us- as a repressive leader.

HOW TO SECURE PEACE WITH CHINA— DETERRENCE OR DIALOGUE?

There is thus a clear fault line in Taiwanese politics. The KMT still has its electoral base in the more than one million Chinese who came to Taiwan with Chiang in 1949. In addition, there are several hundred thousand Taiwanese working in China, although this number has dropped significantly under China's strict covid regulations.

There are many Taiwanese businesspeople with major economic interests in China. Politically, they are also mainly oriented towards the KMT, which promotes economic relations with the mainland. Their economic interests are at stake when relations with China deteriorate.

Therefore, Eric Chu criticizes the DPP government's lack of contact with China, where the KMT promotes dialogue and negotiation with China. "Dialogue is not naive," Eric emphasizes. He is fully aware that China under Xi Jinping is more difficult to negotiate with but adds: "What is the alternative?" other than to try the path of dialogue. Eric adds that trade ensures Taiwan's economic prosperity.

At the same time, KMT leaders understand that Taiwanese voters are not in favor of a return to KMT President Ma Ying-jeou's (2008–2016) unconditional engagement policy with China. His many agreements with China were met with widespread popular opposition in 2014. A demonstrating crowd occupied the parliament when another far-reaching trade and cooperation agreement with China was about to be approved. The protesters got their demands through. The agreement was shelved, even though the KMT had a majority in parliament. The incident is referred to as the Sunflower Revolution because a local florist set up sunflowers outside the parliament in support of the protesters. For many in Taiwanese civil society, it was a landmark event.

There is another fault line in Taiwanese politics: the DPP government's response to China's aggression is to deter China by rearming and relying more on US support and military equipment, while the KMT turns the matter on its head. Rearmament—without dialogue—is the road to war, says Eric Chu.

WILL THE US PROTECT TAIWAN MILITARILY?

An additional political fault line is the role of the US. Is it a protector, or does Taiwan risk being involuntarily caught up in a great power conflict with China?

The DPP government sees the US as the guarantor of Taiwan's security. Therefore, the Tsai government is pleased with Biden's commitment that the US is willing to defend Taiwan militarily.

The KMT contains different voices. For example, former party leader Hung Hsiu-chu criticized Nancy Pelosi's visit to Taiwan. The visit left Taiwan with nothing but trouble, Hung argued in the Taiwanese press.

When I ask Eric Chu, he is more diplomatic and emphasizes that Pelosi was welcome. KMT also questions whether the US would ever drop Taiwan again. Here, history and President Nixon's abrupt turn from Chiang Kai-shek to Mao haunt them.

Another example that supports the fear of the US using Taiwan as a theater of war is the issue of US military supplies, particularly landmines. A headline in an article from a KMT-funded think tank translates roughly as follows: "Are US munitions being stockpiled in Taiwan to ensure Taiwan's destruction?" And the author, a former Taiwanese admiral, continues throughout the article his assessment that Tsai does not care about the safety of the people, but places US landmines everywhere—even in the cities, endangering the general population.

There is likely a broader segment of voters than just KMT core voters who are skeptical of the US, especially among young people. A poll conducted in February 2023 asked Taiwanese whether the US could push Taiwan into a war with China, which 38% agreed. And 44 percent were worried that Taiwan could be used as the US's "pawn". There is a US skepticism in the population that the KMT can benefit from—in this January 2024 elections and onwards.

The US skepticism is further substantiated when I spoke with Puma Shen in January 2023, a Taiwanese researcher on

Chinese disinformation. He also highlights US skepticism as one of the areas which China's propaganda is targeting in the run-up to Taiwan's next presidential election. The goal is to reinforce existing skepticism or circulate false and semi-false stories that capitalize on that US distrust. This has a broad cross-party impact, including among young people who spend a lot of time on social media. Later in the year, Puma Shen changes career and runs for parliament for DPP and himself faces the election campaigns.

CAN TAIWAN'S MULTI-PARTY DEMOCRACY HANDLE CHINA'S PRESSURE?

When the political temperature is high in Taiwan, DPP supporters accuse the KMT of being directly allied with the communists in Beijing, while KMT voters see DPP supporters as crazy independence-seeking forces that jeopardize the country's existence by prodding China to go to war. It's hard to see the compromise or middle ground in the polarization playing out in both traditional and social media. The split is reminiscent of the one that has taken place in the US, where each political camp has its own truth.

On top of this, Taiwan is bombarded with China's interference both in the form of disinformation on social media and through influencing politicians and businesspeople. This reinforces the gap.

China seeks to pressure Taiwanese voters to elect a China-friendly candidate. And if that fails, China's troll armies try to destabilize the entire system, making Taiwan's democracy look messy and chaotic.

However, even with the difficult framework conditions in mind, I am reasonably optimistic about Taiwan's political cohesion—also after my meetings in the different political camps and with Taiwanese voters.

Behind the disagreement, both parties share a common pride in being part of a democratic system. Eric Chu underlined that both parties fight politically and fiercely against each other leading up to an election, but the next day they are ready to work together as a democratic society.

I'm experiencing Taiwan's democracy and the two parties up close and personal as I cover the local elections on November 26, 2022. I attend a young, progressive female DPP candidate's political election event on the Friday evening before the election. It takes place as a city walk with music and voter debate through a megaphone. To ensure a festive atmosphere, there are free shots for the participants.

On election night, I'm at a celebration at KMT headquarters after it becomes clear that Chiang Wan-and has been elected mayor of Taipei. Wan-an, young and charismatic, is the great-grandson—albeit illegitimate—of authoritarian leader Chiang Kai-shek. "He is the future," a KMT supporter assures me. His election is certainly a sign that Taiwan's democracy can accommodate great differences.

At both events, voter engagement is huge, and when I think of languishing Danish political debates at the public library, democracy in Taiwan seems more energetic and livelier.

In conclusion, I find it hard to see China's attempt at peaceful "reunification" by manipulating Taiwan's political system succeeding. Taiwan's political resilience remains solid across party lines.

CHAPTER 4

Taiwanese fighters in battle for Ukraine

The courage and sacrifice of the Ukrainian people in the face of the Russian invasion has inspired people all over the world. Also in Taiwan, even though the country is thousands of kilometers away on the other side of the globe. The Ukraine war has given the feeling that the front line has moved closer to Taiwan.

A large autocratic neighbor has invaded a smaller neighbor. It sounds all too close to home for the Taiwanese living with the tense situation in the Taiwan Strait and China's military threats.

Popular support for Ukraine is strong. Many Taiwanese raise money or participate in support demonstrations. Taiwan Stands With Ukraine is just one of several grassroots organizations that emerged in the wake of Russia's invasion.

But a small group of Taiwanese are taking it a step further. Around ten young men have set off to fight for Ukraine's freedom.

While in Taiwan, I managed to get in touch with several of those who have fought in Ukraine. These people's stories, in my opinion, emphasize the common struggle better than hashtags and official speeches.

In Taipei, I meet Tony Lu, who spent three months fighting at the front east of Izium. I also meet Jack, who also spent a few months at the front. I never get to meet Jonathan Tseng, who died in battle, but I follow his funeral and his final journey back to Taiwan.

FROM HUALIEN TO THE FRONTLINE OF EASTERN UKRAINE

It happens on a Wednesday. November 2, 2022, a 25-year-old man falls on the front lines in battle against Russian forces in Ukraine. For young Ukrainian men, this has unfortunately become commonplace, but this soldier was Taiwanese. His name was Jonathan (Sheng-guang) Tseng and he was born on September 12, 1997 in Hualien, a small town in Taiwan. At the age of 20, he enlisted in the Taiwanese military and left in 2021 after four years of service.

Where Jonathan joins this story is in August 2022, when he heads to Ukraine and joins international forces in the defense against Russia. It will be his first and only visit to Europe.

I scroll through his social media. Photos from before and during the fighting in Ukraine. Facebook and Instagram have become the diary—and obituary—of the electronic age. On September 25, 2022, Jonathan posts a new cover photo—for the last time. It's a selfie of him in full combat uniform with a lit cigarette hanging from the corner of his mouth. It must be Marlboro, because he's holding the red pack loosely in his right hand while holding the selfie-ready cell phone in his left. He stands in front of a cabinet with a large mirror. The wall behind is half smashed. The image reeks of war.

In another post, Jonathan proudly shows that he has sewn an insignia with both the Taiwanese and Ukrainian flags on his uniform. The symbolism of a united fight for the two countries and a united fight for freedom is striking.

After Jonathan's death, the Ukrainian authorities organize a memorial service for him, attended by the local mayor. It takes place on a gray day in November 2022 in the western Ukrainian city of Lviv. Inna Sovsun, a Ukrainian member of parliament, tells the press that Jonathan's death was not in vain. "Ukraine will win. And when Taiwan needs support, I think Ukrainians will come, as Tseng came to help in a time of need."

The Taiwanese Ministry of Foreign Affairs has helped bring Jonathan's mother and wife all the way from Taiwan into war-torn Ukraine for the funeral. The last part of the journey is by train from Poland. Russia has closed Ukraine's airspace.

I watch the funeral in Ukraine online. In the church, the mother sits on a chair near the coffin and cries. She holds a Ukrainian flag folded in a triangle. Jonathan's fellow soldiers, young and strong men, fasten the lid on his coffin before six of them in combat uniform carry the coffin out. Outside the church, both Ukrainian and Taiwanese flags are held up by the attendees and mourners.

While I reside in Taiwan at the end of November 2022, Jonathan's urn arrives on a plane with his mother and wife. The wife keeps the urn close to her. The arrival is closely covered by the Taiwanese media. At the airport, a short press conference is held, which I watch.

"I will always be proud of my son," says the mother, tearful in front of the rolling cameras. She continues: "He saw the people, women and children affected by the war. He couldn't stand it. He had to do something… he was ready to sacrifice himself for his beliefs and couldn't live in an unjust world. That's why he went to Ukraine." The mother also mentions that at the funeral in Lviv, she was touched to meet his fellow soldiers. They told her about her son's courage and self-sacrificing behavior on the front line.

I enlist the help of a Taiwanese acquaintance to translate from the press conference at the airport. In a side note, she tells me that Jonathan belonged to the Presbyterian denomination. His first name in Chinese means holy light.

Here on earth, Jonathan brought at least a little light for Ukraine against the darkness of Russia and his ultimate sacrifice fighting for freedom.

TONY BY IZIUM

I know that Jonathan is not the only Taiwanese who has fought in Ukraine, so I try to reach out to others. I ask around among Taiwanese acquaintances, journalists and the Taiwanese Ministry of Foreign Affairs, but without much luck. I also try through Jonathan Tseng's Facebook friends, where I notice several people with military background. But no one responds to my Messenger messages.

I'm at a standstill until I attend a Christmas support event for Ukraine in Taipei in December 2022. I bump into Oleksandr, a Ukrainian military doctor who has just visited Jonathan Tseng's family to offer his personal condolences. Oleksandr shows me a very touching video clip where he, wearing a Ukrainian embroidered shirt, meets Jonathan's family in their village outside Hualien. In the video, Oleksandr sings in Ukrainian and falls to his knees crying in front of Jonathan's family.

On my way out, I come across a Taiwanese man wearing a face mask in the Ukrainian blue and yellow colors that reads "slava Ukraini". We strike up a conversation and take a photo together. "Tony," he introduces himself. As we mess around with our phones to share our double selfie, Tony shows me a series of photos on his phone. It's from the war in Ukraine! Tony himself is in uniform in several photos. I've met my first Taiwanese who fought at the front and came back alive. We agree to meet again so that I can hear his whole story.

We do this later in December on a Friday evening at a restaurant. I have a Taiwanese translator with me, Anita Chang. Tony's English is much better than my Chinese, but still quite limited.

Tony gives me his cell phone so I can flip through his photos and see his footage from three months in Ukraine from March to June 2022. Tony is 34 years old, a former butcher with one year of military service behind him. He explains that he can't be described as one of God's best children, as he used to be a big gambler. However, he was inspired when he heard former Taiwanese Vice President Chen Chien-jen talk about the importance of doing something for others in his life. It resonated with him so much that when Russia started the war against Ukraine, he decided to join. He himself compares Ukraine's situation to that of Taiwan. There is a big country attacking a smaller country. It feels comparable.

Some of Tony's first photos from the end of March are from Poland, from where he traveled by train to Ukraine. Then there are pictures from his stay in Lviv, in Western Ukraine where Tony meets ordinary Ukrainians for the first time—the people whose fate he feels he shares to such an extent that he wants to fight for them.

He tells me that in the early days, he distributed relief aid to Ukrainian internally displaced persons. I ask about the language barrier, as Tony speaks neither Ukrainian nor much English. "Compassion and solidarity don't need a language," he replies. "Another person can feel when you help."

We flip through Tony's photos of new soldier colleagues from his enlistment in the international forces. There are two other Taiwanese among them. One, as he explains, is called Long. But he doesn't meet Jonathan Tseng, who arrives in Ukraine around the same time Tony travels back to Taiwan. But Tony tells me that he nevertheless attended the funeral in Hualien to honor Jonathan.

As Tony points to photos of himself from Ukraine, he pulls at his cheeks. I don't understand the gesture. But it's to illustrate that he was fat while he was in Ukraine. It was so cold, he says, so he had to eat a lot. His stay in Ukraine was also his first encounter with snow and cold. In Taipei, where we meet, the December temperature is 15 degrees and on a sunny day it's well above 20 degrees.

From April onwards, Tony is at the front near Izium, east of Kharkiv. I see photos and videos from there. I hear the sound of gunfire. The sound of artillery. He tells me that their task was all about defense and holding their positions. The Ukrainian military had not yet received long-range artillery from the Americans to attack and pressure the Russian positions.

Tony takes his phone back. There's a clip he's looking for. He wants to show it to me. It's a video, not many seconds long, but terrifying. Tony is in a trench; there is background noise. He carefully films out from the trench. A large piece of Russian artillery—a bomb, civilians might say—has landed close to Tony, but the bomb hasn't exploded. It just sits there, ominous and potentially deadly. Tony explains to me that before that experience he wasn't afraid of anything, but the bomb was very close. Now he describes himself as a little bit religious and very happy that he survived. Meanwhile, Adele's hit song "Hello from the other side" floats through the room, as we talk. The restaurant's background music is eerily appropriate.

A couple of times I scroll too quickly through Tony's many photos from the war. He stops me. "He's dead," he says laconically, pointing to a fellow soldier. An Australian. Tony sends me a YouTube video about him afterwards. He was referred to as the "Australian ninja". More photos: a Colombian. A Ukrainian. Also dead. From around the globe, but united in common defense against Russia. And now also united in death in Ukraine.

I ask Tony if he thinks his fellow surviving soldiers will come to defend Taiwan if China attacks. He is convinced they will. He takes it very literally and shows me a Facebook post from a woman in military uniform and Tony next to her, where she writes that she will defend Taiwan if China attacks. It's the people-to-people version of NATO's Article 5 to protect each other. Tony is also convinced that Ukraine will win against Russian supremacy, especially if the rest of the world continues to support them.

Tony runs out of money in Ukraine. There is a limited salary for the international soldiers, but a Taiwanese businessman who is impressed by Tony's bravery, arranges to pay for his return to Taiwan.

"What can Ukraine's war teach Taiwan?" I ask. Resilience is the key word, Tony says. "It's about not giving up and keeping your courage up." That's why Tony also supports extending Taiwanese conscription to one year from the current four months. "Most Taiwanese hear the Chinese military planes flying closer and closer to Taiwan," he says. Taiwan needs to be even more prepared, as Taiwanese soldiers cannot withdraw to train in another country. Unlike Ukrainian soldiers, who have been trained in Poland and other European countries. As Tony concludes: "Many Ukrainians didn't want to go to war either. They were forced to. To defend their homes."

It's Boxing Day 2022, but in Taiwan it's an ordinary Monday. I've gotten in contact with another Taiwanese who fought in Ukraine near Butja. Jack is his English name. We meet at a café in Da'an, Taipei. Jack is wearing a beautiful coat, and underneath he's wearing a stylish gray turtleneck sweater. He has fine features and looks more like a menswear model than a soldier. But he has done his military service in the Taiwanese military. He is 29 years old.

I ask my obligatory why question. Jack says that Ukrainians are just like Taiwanese. "If we don't stop Russia in Ukraine, China will invade Taiwan."

He doesn't tell his family that he is departing for Ukraine. His father and brothers only discover after he has already spent several weeks in Ukraine. His father got angry, he explains. Jack has replied to his dad's earlier messages that he was on a work trip in Taiwan, when he was already in Ukraine. Jack has a company where he imports and sells coffee to cafés and hotels. His father had wanted him to become a doctor like him.

It's clear to me that Jack comes from a different and more affluent background than Tony. His family thinks it is crazy rather than heroic that he has volunteered in the defense of Ukraine. They don't see how defending Ukraine has any connection to protecting Taiwan's freedom.

Jack tells me that the Taiwanese representative office in Poland had carried out an evacuation of Taiwanese citizens from Ukraine just before he entered Ukraine in March 2022. He contacted the office, which advised him against going to Ukraine. Jack, like Jonathan or Tony, has also never been to Europe before arriving in Ukraine in the middle of a war.

On the road into Ukraine, Jack meets a Canadian who is on his way out—away from the front and the war. "Don't," he tells Jack. "You have no idea what you're getting into." Jack confirms the latter. He has no idea what he's getting into. Not even on a practical level, as he has to provide food to Ukrainian internal refugees. He has no idea what they eat. He is used to Taiwanese cooking. There's not much to choose from, so potatoes it becomes.

At the front, Jack joins a Georgian company near Butja, the city synonymous with Russia's war crimes. For Jack, meeting the Georgians also introduces him to a new—and unknown to him—chapter of European history. The Georgian fighters see their fight for Ukraine as part of their own country's defense against Russia. "2008," Jack says to me with a knowing nod, adding, "Russia's invasion of Georgia". He is impressed to serve with two Georgians. It's father and son fighting together.

Jack also tells me of confusion about his own nationality and background. His passport, like all Taiwanese, has the official title "Republic of China" (skip back to chapter 2 if you need to get that story straight). He is asked by Ukrainian soldiers if he likes Xi Jinping because his passport says China. Jack must provide the history. He is Taiwanese. And no, he is not a fan of Xi Jinping.

I ask if he otherwise met understanding for Taiwan in Ukraine. Jack shows me his war photos on his phone. In one photo, Jack is in military uniform, and in another photo, he stands with other soldiers. They are holding a Ukrainian and Taiwanese flag with Taiwan written in black marker on the red color of the flag.

I also ask Jack if he thinks the Ukrainians and other international soldiers will come to Taiwan's rescue if the country is attacked. "Yes," he says immediately. "We will meet again either in Ukraine or in Taiwan," the other soldiers said as a farewell greeting as Jack left Ukraine. Jack adds thoughtfully to me: "I just hope we don't meet in Taiwan, because that means we're in a really bad situation."

The war has taken its toll on him. When Nancy Pelosi visits Taiwan in August 2022, Jack has just returned from Ukraine. When he witnesses China's military exercises along Taiwan, he sees it as a parallel to Russia's exercises along the Ukraine border—a prelude to war. He tells me he goes into war mode and gathers survival gear. His family and friends think he's overreacting. They are right. The war didn't come—this time.

Jack mentions that the Taiwanese appreciate comfort and material prosperity. For most of them, the thought of having to defend their country may seem distant. Taiwan has lived with the threat of war for decades, but many have forgotten that war could happen.

Jack's message to China is simple: "Let's live our way. Let's live in peace. There is no need to start a war."

CHAPTER 5

The porcupine strategy. Can Taiwan defend itself against China?

"Ukraine today, Taiwan tomorrow." That is what many Taiwanese wrote on social media right after Russia invaded Ukraine. The message was shared with a mixture of gloomy prediction and nervousness.

Since Nancy Pelosi's visit in August 2022 and China's largest military exercises in decades, the Chinese military has been trying to establish a "new normal" with almost constant military approaches into the Taiwanese air defense zone with its jet fighters. Chinese and Taiwanese jet fighters on the wings have become part of the background noise for the Taiwanese population—especially in the southern part of the island. I experience this myself while staying in Taiwan. The number of Chinese unwanted approaches has doubled over the past year, according to the Taiwanese authorities.

This chapter is about a possible war, a war that no civilized person wants, but a war that Xi Jinping is threatening to launch.

Therefore, I review China's various options for attacking Taiwan militarily. This could be the large-scale war with a D-Day-style invasion of Taiwan's beaches, a crippling missile attack, a "seize-an-island" scenario, or a Chinese quarantine or blockade of Taiwan by sea.

I have discussed such scenarios with Taiwanese politicians and military officials, as well as with US military and diplomatic sources from my network in Washington DC.

Against this background, I track Taiwan's military resilience. The key question is whether Taiwan can transform itself -military speaking -into a porcupine—that can curl up and greet the opponent with impenetrable hard spikes. The porcupine terminology is used by American and, increasingly, Taiwanese military experts to describe the deterrent effect that Taiwan should have on China if it is adequately prepared for all possible attacks.

CHINA-TAIWAN MILITARY SNAPSHOT

In Taipei, I met with former Vice Minister of Defense, Admiral and Commander of the Taiwanese Navy, Chen Yeong-kang. Admiral Chen remains active in the debate on defense policy issues.

We schedule lunch in central Taipei at the former residence of General Sun Li-jen, who fell from grace in the 1950s under Chiang Kai-shek. For decades, the general was under house arrest in this building, which dates back to Japanese colonial times. The residence has fine wooden facades and an ornate Japanese-style garden and is now a military club.

During lunch, I am shown a PowerPoint presentation filled with detailed satellite photos and maps that Admiral Chen has compiled to illustrate the differences and similarities between Ukraine and Taiwan's military situation. Admiral Chen's analysis puts perspectives on the different possible war scenarios.

On paper, the balance of power between Taiwan and China looks very unequal. China has used its economic muscle to build the world's second largest military over the last two decades. Its air force is ten times the size of Taiwan's, and the Chinese navy is now larger than the American, although the quality is still somewhat lower. China's missiles—thousands of them—have their tips pointed at Taiwan.

A key element of China's long-standing military buildup is training to take Taiwan. China's military, officially called the People's Liberation Army (PLA), refers to it as a "historic mission", precisely because throughout history and during the Cold War, military attempts to take Taiwan in 1949 and 1958 failed.

The military threat picture looks overwhelming—and has some similarities to Ukraine's military disparity with Russia. Based on that, some conclude that Taiwan doesn't stand a chance. But that's too quick a conclusion. Even with its much larger forces, it won't necessarily be easy for the Chinese military to invade Taiwan. The costs, both militarily and economically, would be extremely high. And in the analysis of many, including Admiral Chen, the Chinese military is not ready for an invasion. Yet.

CAN XI UNDER PRESSURE TAKE INSPIRATION FROM PUTIN?

Many analysts assume that Xi Jinping is a rational decision-maker who considers the huge costs that a major military attack would entail for China. Ergo, Xi will not attack. But after 2022 and Putin's attack on Ukraine, many policymakers feel less confident in that analysis.

Internal discontent and instability in China could tilt Xi's calculus.

I'm in Taiwan as many Chinese take to the streets protesting strict Covid rules at the end of November 2022. In private conversations, I hear several top Taiwanese officials expressing concern about what happens if Xi is further pressured at home by popular discontent. He might need a war to rally the Chinese people behind him.

Putin's example is frightening. He launched a major war against Ukraine without his military being ready and capable enough and without expecting the economic costs that the EU and G7 countries' sanctions against Russia would create.

With that in mind, it's hard to gauge how Xi Jinping under domestic pressure might weigh his options in the coming period.

Therefore, first and foremost the Taiwanese, but also the rest of the world, will have to deal with the possibility of a war that nobody wants. After Ukraine, "never say never" is a new premise, as a Taiwanese military analyst put it to me.

D-DAY IN THE TAIWAN STRAIT

A Chinese invasion attack will start with missiles and air strikes to smash Taiwan's air defenses and navy. In missile range, there is a short distance across the Strait. It doesn't take much longer than brewing a barista coffee to send a missile from China to Taiwan. Only as Taiwan's air defenses and navy are destroyed can a Chinese invasion fleet be sent across the Taiwan Strait.

Here's a big military difference from Ukraine. Admiral Chen points to one of his maps on the PowerPoint. "Do you see the difference?" he asks rhetorically. That's the blue moat around Taiwan: the sea. The blue ocean also represents the difference in supply lines. Ukraine has many supply lines on land. Taiwan has none.

Ukraine has land borders with the aggressor country Russia, but Ukraine also has borders with several friendly countries such as Poland, Slovakia and Romania. This offers some advantages. Ukrainian war refugees can be moved across borders. They are under protection elsewhere in Europe. Ukrainian soldiers can be trained in neighboring countries. Essential Western weapons supplies can flow in effortlessly from the west.

It's a different story for Taiwan. As Admiral Chen states: "There is no refugee corridor for Taiwan." Taiwanese refugees would have nowhere else to go. The Taiwanese military cannot be trained in neighboring countries to be re-deployed in combat if China has already launched an attack. Finally, it could be very difficult to get weapons and other supplies into Taiwan if China blocks the sea lanes around the island. Even for the US Navy, it could be a major task.

But the sea is also in Taiwan's favor. The Taiwan Strait is unpredictable with strong winds. Typhoon season limits the time of year China can attack. Pronounced tides also limit the time of day to strike. Finally, Taiwan's coast is full of rocks and cliffs with few flat beaches for China's military to embark on.

Chinese military manuals, which American military analyst Ian Easton has described in his books, mention about 14 beaches on Taiwan where a D-Day-like attack could be deployed. Taiwan's military planners are equally aware of these beaches. They meticulously know their few vulnerable stretches. On the rest of Taiwan's coast, an invasion force would be met by mountains and slopes. Some beaches are plastered with coastal defenses—and now also in several places with

Danish-built offshore wind turbines, making it harder to land a Chinese force as large as that required for an invasion.

Taiwan also has the defensive advantage. A military rule of thumb is that an attacker must have at least three times as many forces as the defending party. Taiwan has a standing army of around 169,000 but can quickly draw on and call up reserves. The Taiwanese force numbers will be reinforced over the coming years with the increased conscription.

Internal Chinese military manuals therefore also mention the possibility of deploying a force of up to one million men. It's a scenario the world hasn't seen since D-Day in 1944. This makes the war in Ukraine, as horrific as it is, pale in military terms.

A war of aggression against Taiwan would likely involve the US in direct military confrontation. President Biden has been clear in his commitment that the US will defend Taiwan if China attacks. This puts a China-Taiwan war in a different league from the Ukraine war, where the US only supports from the sidelines with military equipment. It would rapidly escalate into the great power conflict of the 21st century, and for the first time, two nuclear powers would be in direct military conflict with incalculable consequences. For themselves. And for the rest of the world.

In addition to the US, Japan can be expected to be involved in such a major regional war. During the Chinese military exercises in August 2022, a Chinese missile crossed over Taiwan and landed, albeit in the depths of the ocean, but close to Japan.

Japanese soil—mostly on the southern island of Okinawa, close to Taiwan—is home to the US bases and navy. Both are being heavily upgraded these years.

Following the war in Ukraine, Japan's Prime Minister Kishida has announced that the country's defense budget will increase to two percent. As Japan remains the world's third-largest economy, these are large sums of money. As a novelty, Japan, which is governed by a pacifist constitution, is developing an offensive missile capability. This can defend Japan, but also provide a response to China if Taiwan is attacked.

In early 2023, the US think tank Center for Strategic and International Studies (CSIS) in Washington DC released a simulation game about a possible war over Taiwan. In some ways, the conclusion is comforting. The US and Taiwan will win in almost every scenario. But for both Taiwan and the US, the military costs would be enormous, such as the loss of two US aircraft carriers and up to ten naval vessels and fighter jets in huge numbers. The assumptions in the simulation were that the Taiwanese people would be willing to fight, and that the US would become militarily involved in the conflict early on.

Admiral Chen, who I meet with shortly after the simulation game's release, is skeptical about parts of the scenario and its assumptions. He agrees with the basic premise that Taiwan and the US will win. But Chen is convinced that the casualties will be much higher.

Chen mentions that the scenario excludes an important variable, which is the evacuation of US citizens from both Taiwan and China. Such an evacuation would be like the canary in the coal mine: a signal that the Americans assess, based on their unrivaled intelligence, that war is coming. Just as the Americans evacuated their citizens in Ukraine before the Russian invasion began. Such an evacuation—and a signal of impending war—would set off a negative spiral in global stock markets. Such a course of events might cause China to reassess their plans when the economy is already plummeting before an attack, Chen explains.

THE TARGETED HIT—"ONE STRIKE, AND YOU ARE OUT"

There is a smaller version of the large-scale invasion scenario where China would only use targeted missile strikes and limited force. It is reminiscent of the scenario that Putin first envisioned in Ukraine in February 2022, with a surprise attack and the swift elimination of President Volodymyr Zelenskyy and his political leadership. As we know, that did not succeed.

"A Chinese precision-guided missile hitting the right spot in Taipei could paralyze us," explains a military commander I meet with. I infer that he means a Chinese missile attack on the presidential building and Taiwan's political leadership in the government district in central Taipei.

Another senior official in the national security apparatus elaborates to me that "Xi Jinping's lesson from Ukraine is that China must win quickly over Taiwan, otherwise there will be US-led sanctions by democratic countries and huge economic losses."

However, a closer analysis of the feasibility of such a paralyzing missile strike by China appears to be more wishful thinking than a genuine military option.

China would have to follow up with elements of a classic military invasion with boots on the ground. Even if the Taiwanese political leadership were taken out to in a surprise attack, it is not at all certain, it would lead to a quick surrender.

A missile attack on Taiwan's leadership could be expected to rally the Taiwanese people in resistance. In such a situation, no Taiwanese would believe that any kind of negotiated solution could be reached with China. And then China is faced with a united, combative and defiant Taiwan.

On a gray day in January 2023, I'm standing on the Kinmen archipelago. I'm still in Taiwan, but I can look across to the high-rise buildings of Xiamen—the Chinese coastal city in Fujian province, where Xi Jinping was provincial governor from 1999 to 2002. Here, China and Taiwan are only a few kilometers apart—about the length of the Golden Gate Bridge.

Military analysts highlighted the possibility that China could take Kinmen or one of the other islands like Matsu, both of which are close to China's coast. The possibility of this scenario was reinforced by China sending drones over Kinmen in the fall of 2022 filming Taiwanese soldiers from the air. The footage was deployed on Chinese social media to poke fun at Taiwan's defense of Kinmen. A shot of a Taiwanese soldier shouting and throwing rocks at the drone, went viral. However, the Chinese drone flyovers stopped, when the Taiwanese military managed to shoot down a drone.

If China seizes Kinmen or Matsu, it would be comparable to when Putin took Crimea in 2014. Such a "seize an island" maneuver would test whether both Taiwan and the US would be willing to go to war over a few square kilometers of island that is far away from Taiwan's main island.

On the economic front, it would reveal whether there was a willingness in the US and other democratic countries such as in Europe to implement sanctions against China in response.

A takeover of Kinmen would hold historical symbolism for China. In 1949, Mao's communist army lost heavily to the nationalist army on Kinmen. In 1958, China attacked Kinmen again with massive artillery fire. But the island held out both times.

During my visit, I pass several military memorials on Kinmen, where the fallen soldiers and their heroic efforts are honored.

Until the end of the Cold War, Kinmen was administered by Taiwan's military. There were over 100,000 Taiwanese troops there—often buried in huge tunnel systems. I visit one such tunnel system, which now serves as a museum, paradoxically also for Chinese tourists visiting from the mainland.

Today, Taiwan's soldiers on the island number just a few thousand. The most active effort I observe is a group of soldiers—they look like conscripts—sweeping a street in the morning.

But even in a limited "seize an island" scenario, this could lead to a broader military conflict between China, Taiwan and the US. US policymakers also recall the 2014 invasion of Crimea. In hindsight, they see that their limited response made Putin think he got away with it. Based on that learning, even in a small landgrab scenario, the US reaction could be tough. The US understands the parallels to how China—like Russia—is testing its red lines and willingness to stand ground.

Thus, there is a great risk of escalation for China and limited gain by occupying an island.

In addition, the Chinese economic presence, especially in Kinmen, is making the island increasingly dependent on China. Why fire a shot if you can defeat your opponent without a fight? I write more about that in chapter 8.

THE BLOCKADE OR QUARANTINE SCENARIO
AND THE HUNGRY PORCUPINE

"A blockade is clearly the most likely. And where Taiwan is most vulnerable," Admiral Chen points out to me. He underlines

Taiwan's isolated location in the sea. If China blocks access to Taiwan by sea, the island is in trouble.

It all comes down to whether the US Navy is ready to match China's and can keep the sea lanes open. Otherwise, Taiwan could quickly run out of energy, food and medical products. Especially when it comes to energy, Taiwan is dependent on supplies from the outside world. There is way too little energy produced on the island to be self-sufficient.

A full blockade would be considered a war scenario, not least because of the economic costs. Passage through the Taiwan Strait is a shipping artery for world trade. And Taiwan's central role in the computer chip industry means that a full blockade would bring global technology supply chains to a standstill.

But lighter blockades or selective quarantines are part of China's toolbox too. These could target Taiwan's energy supply or other vital products. China could also operate in the grey zone or hybrid space by deploying coast guard ships or private fishing vessels as part of such efforts. Such "civilian" means have been used in the past by China in the South China Sea against neighboring countries.

This would make it harder for Taiwan and the outside world to classify such a step as a military action. That would in turn make a military response from Taiwan and the US appear escalatory. The use of civilian means is an effective way to shift the threshold in China's favor. Such methods help to wear down Taiwan's resilience.

Hybrid approaches would fit well with China's anaconda strategy of slowly but surely strangling Taiwan's connections to the outside world. As Admiral Chen tells me, a starving porcupine is not worth much in battle. He's referring to a situation where Taiwan's military and civilians are short of supplies from food to energy.

Admiral Chen tells me that he sees Taiwan's greatest weakness in the economic and not the military sphere. China is the largest trading partner. There is no quick substitute for that. China always has the option of using market access as a means of blackmail.

CAN TAIWAN TURN INTO AN ATTACK-PROOF PORCUPINE?

"No one wants a war," says Taiwan's President Tsai Ing-wen in a speech to the Taiwanese people, but "to prevent a war, you must prepare for one". On the military front, Taiwan is conducting a military build-up to deter China.

A key lesson from Ukraine's stalwart defense against Russia is the willingness of the people to defend themselves. Several Taiwanese explain to me, that the older generation has fought inside Taiwan for their freedom against the former authoritarian regime of Chiang Kai-shek. They will not give up that freedom again without a fight.

The Taiwanese also know that US military support depends on their own willingness to fight and stand their ground. This is the difference from Afghanistan to Ukraine. If the Ukrainian government had fallen or Zelenskyy had fled at the beginning of the war, Western military support would never have materialized. Tsai Ing-wen's spokeswoman Kolas Yotaka said that "we have to defend ourselves, no one else will fight for our democracy like we can".

Just prior to New Year 2023 President Tsai Ing-wen announces an extension of military conscription from 4 to 12 months. With this announcement, she sends a signal to both

China and the US about Taiwan's increased willingness to defend itself. But as she emphasizes in her speech, it is a difficult decision.

Conscription has been unpopular among Taiwanese youth for years—many of whom vote for her party, the Democratic Progressive Party. Had it not been for the Ukraine war, it would have been politically unthinkable to extend conscription just one year before a crucial presidential election in January 2024.

But the Ukraine war and China's military exercises are doing their part to change the mood. However, the content of the conscription reform will be crucial. I hear from several young Taiwanese that they have been assigned to useless activities such as sweeping during conscription. That's why the President goes into detail in her speech. Training will no longer be with a bayonet, but with drones or Stinger missiles; in other words, modern warfare. And military training that supports an asymmetric way of holding out against a Chinese attack.

Taiwan can never rearm enough to match China's soldiers, aircraft and naval vessels. Therefore, it's all about focusing on asymmetric responses, i.e. a David versus Goliath mindset. It's about using the stone sling against a larger opponent. It could be like how Ukraine's military has successfully used drones and other unmanned systems against the Russian invaders.

There are many suggestions for strengthening Taiwan's asymmetric capabilities. During a visit to Taiwan in April 2023, former US National Security Advisor to President Trump, Robert O'Brien, suggested that the Taiwanese civilian population should be armed with one million automatic weapons to deter China. This proposal does not go down well in Taiwan, which, like Denmark, has very restrictive gun laws for civilians.

In this area, there is a lively discussion, often behind closed doors, both within the Taiwanese military and with American interlocutors about what exactly the best asymmetric strategy looks like. Is it urban combat with smaller decentralized units? If it is urban combat, does it still make sense to use tanks, which the Taiwanese army would like to acquire more of. Hidden inside the discussion about the right asymmetric strategy, lies a classical funding battle between army, navy and air force, who all want their share of new equipment from the increasing military budget.

However, a Taiwanese military researcher dryly lays out the situation to me that Taiwan's military strategy is ultimately determined by what equipment the US is willing to sell to Taiwan—its sole foreign provider.

On military sales, the Ukraine war has effects on Taiwan. Deliveries from the US have slowed down on products such as Javelin anti-tank missiles that have been sent to Ukraine. And in December 2023 when the US Congress held up military aid to Ukraine, it also affected Taiwan whose funding was part of the US administration's proposal to Congress.

AW!—THE TAIWANESE PORCUPINE STINGS

Following my interviews about the military situation in Taiwan, I draw a couple of conclusions.

One is uplifting. It is easy for China to threaten Taiwan militarily, but difficult for China to invade the island, even with China's military superiority in numbers. At the same time, Ukraine's defense against a superior opponent is also encouraging news for Taiwan.

In addition, Taiwan is strengthening its military resilience. Maybe the porcupine hasn't raised all its quills yet. But they do sting. The population is by and large behind a bigger and stronger defense.

The second observation I draw is depressing. If a conflict does happen, it could result in mass casualties, much greater than what we see in the Russia-Ukraine war. With the US engaged, it would potentially be a World War III. Economically devastating, also in the European economy, because Taiwan and China play critical roles in the world economy.

Personally, I'm most worried about some kind of quarantine or smaller blockade scenario. This could happen as early as the Taiwanese and US presidential elections in 2024.

It could start with a Chinese military exercise which could slide into a blockade. A military researcher I speak with emphasizes that China's military exercises after Pelosi's visit de facto briefly blockaded Taiwan.

Eventually, a prolonged military "exercise" could slide into a real war. This is comparable to Putin's many military exercises near Ukraine. China's military exercises in response to Tsai Ing-wen's meeting with Kevin McCarthy in April 2023 should also be seen in this light. Both as a warning and as a training round. We get used to China's military drills—until one day it actually is the real thing.

There is also the danger of an accidental mishap that triggers a conflict. The Taiwan Strait is increasingly filled with military aircraft, ships and submarines. A military conflict can be ignited by an accident or an unplanned clash between Chinese and Taiwanese or American aircraft, ships or submarines.

When the US shot down a suspected Chinese spy balloon in February 2023, it became clear how short the fuse is—also in Washington.

CHAPTER 6

Civil Defense—Taiwan's Black Bear Warriors

"Ow, it hurts," a young man screams. He's lying on the floor, bloody and battered from gunshot wounds. I see the blood pulsing out. Two women are kneeling. They are administering first aid. One cleans his wounds. The other prepares a tourniquet, which they tie around his thigh to stop the bleeding. A little further away, another injured person is moaning.

This is neither an accident nor the beginning of a war. It takes place on a peaceful Sunday in January 2023 in Taipei on the ninth floor of a modest apartment building. It's an extended first aid course organized by the civil society organization Forward Alliance.

I've written to the founder Enoch Wu and was allowed to attend. Today, the students learn how to stop bleeding in wounded people. In addition to the volunteers playing injured, there are also some artificial arms with bloody wounds for the students to practice on.

The course is very popular. It's sold out. Therefore, I find myself in a small room with 60 people in a cramped space. The noise from both the injured and the participants is deafening. I manage to spot Enoch Wu, who is wearing a blue T-shirt with the Forward Alliance logo and the motto "I can Help."

In addition to being the initiator of this project, Enoch is also a political candidate for the Democratic Progressive Party, DPP. I've been trying to meet with him since I arrived in Taiwan in November 2022, but he has been busy campaigning for a special election for a seat in Taiwan's parliament, where he narrowly lost to the KMT candidate on January 8, 2023. In 2022, Enoch was included in the US Times magazine's top 100 list of future leaders. He is a charismatic and handsome man with a large group of especially female followers among his over 330,000 Facebook followers.

We sit down in a back room, where we can still hear the screams of the wounded volunteers. I ask Enoch why he initiated this civilian training and what effect the war in Ukraine has had.

The initial goal of the initiative was to build more resilience in the population in the event of natural disasters such as earthquakes or typhoons and, in the worst-case scenario, a war situation. To cover Taiwan's 23 million inhabitants, there are only 16,000 firefighters who are responsible for both firefighting and responding to accidents, Enoch explains. There is a need for a strong civil society that can also step in. The trainers at the workshop are from the firefighter corps. In a major crisis situation, they would also be responsible for working with civilians.

Forward Alliance also runs courses that provide the Taiwanese with basic self-defense and crisis management skills. "Write down the phone numbers of your family members and arrange a meeting place in advance in case of a crisis," is one of the practical tips, Enoch shares.

In 2020, when Forward Alliance started, they offered fewer courses, but since the invasion of Ukraine, courses have been running weekly. And the seats fill up quickly.

Defense readiness, Enoch says, is basically the biggest challenge facing Taiwanese society over the next decades. He emphasizes the need for strong cooperation between the military, government and civil society: "The foundation is the people's resilience and will to resist," he says. But he emphasizes that Forward Alliance only provides civilian training: "We don't teach people how to throw Molotov cocktails."

Enoch sees an active civil society as Taiwan's strength. Civil society has driven Taiwan's democracy forward with the demand for freedom of speech, the democracy movement, nuclear resistance, and the legalization of same sex marriage in 2019.

This strong community involvement is also part of Enoch's personal story from childhood. Enoch highlights how he got his early training in the 1990s by collecting signatures for a referendum against the construction of a new nuclear power plant. A nuclear-free Taiwan is a key issue for the DPP and its voter base. The last nuclear power plant is expected to close in 2025.

Enoch says that Forward Alliance has trained around 4–5,000 students. The ambition is to open offices in cities other than Taipei. 86,000 well-trained first responders are Forward Alliance's goal. When achieved, that would constitute a civilian counterpart for every one of Taiwan's 86,000 police and firefighters. This will significantly increase the country's resilience, says Enoch.

Forward Alliance is funded by donations and participation fees. It costs 150 Taiwanese dollars (just over 4 euros) to join, so it's affordable for most people. The organization receives no external funding that can quickly scale up their activities.

THE BLACK BEAR WARRIORS WITH MONEY IN THEIR POCKETS

The war in Ukraine has sparked several civil society initiatives to defend Taiwan. Another is the Kuma Academy, which has a black bear holding a rifle as its logo. Kuma is much better funded than Forward Alliance.

Computer chip billionaire Robert Tsao, who you will also get to know in the next chapter, donated three billion Taiwan dollars (around 90 million euros) to Taiwan's defense in 2022. And over half of Tsao's donation has been directed to Kuma Academy.

I have the chance to meet with Robert Tsao and hear his perspectives on Taiwan's defense. We meet up in his beautiful apartment overlooking Da'an Park. These are expensive square meters in Taipei.

Robert, who is in his seventies with wavy chalk-white hair, returned to Taiwan in 2022 under considerable media fanfare. He had been living in Singapore until then. He had given up his Taiwanese citizenship due to a lawsuit. Previously, as a businessman and computer chip manufacturer, he has also successfully conducted business in China.

Tsao got his Taiwanese passport back and has assumed a new identity as a frontline Taiwan defender. Appearing for interviews with international media, he wears a bulletproof vest to emphasize how dangerous the situation is for Taiwan. When we meet, however, it's a little more relaxed, both without protective gear and without shoes on, as Tsao's apartment is neatly decorated with Japanese tatami, or reed mats, as flooring.

As we sit down at his table and start our conversation, I notice two Chinese characters tattooed on the front of his fingers. In Taiwan, tattoos are a bit atypical for a businessman.

He tells me that the tattoos are a good icebreaker for him with the younger generation. They show the characters zhi and ding 知定.

Tsao explains to me that his personal turning point was when China started to suppress people and the democracy movement in Hong Kong. Tsao highlights an incident on July 21, 2019, as a watershed moment for him. Chinese-paid thugs attacked ordinary people coming from a demonstration at a subway station in Hong Kong. The police did not intervene in time. "It made me angry," he says, so he wanted to go back to Taiwan to warn about the danger of the nature of the Communist Party of China.

China's aggressive military response to Nancy Pelosi's visit made Tsao even more determined to contribute to Taiwan's defense. According to him, Taiwanese lack self-confidence. It is the will to defend themselves that needs to be strengthened, and this must be coupled with a comprehension that the Communist Party of China cannot be trusted.

Tsao doesn't tell me his political affiliation but his views sound very similar to those I hear from the ruling party DPP. Typically, many Taiwanese businessmen, especially those with business in China, support the Nationalist Party, which stands for continued economic relations with China. Tsao mentions that he is good friends with Foxconn owner Terry Gou, who is much more China-positive and who ran for President of Taiwan in 2024 although he withdrew at the last minute in November 2023.

I ask about Tsao's personal change of heart. I have read that in 2007, he proposed to hold a referendum on whether Taiwan should be part of China. Today, he explains—diplomatically—that the proposal was not because he was in favor of incorporating Taiwan into China, but he only meant to start a democratic debate.

Tsao is part of Taiwan's business elite, who has made fortunes in China to such a degree that the Taiwanese authorities have had him and his—now former—microchip company UMC under examination for illegal transfers of technology to China.

Tsao admits that for many years he believed in the economic reform policy in China. In a reformed and more open China. But not with Xi Jinping at the helm. He is, according to Tsao, an uneducated person who has only read one book, "The Little Red Book"—by Mao. Xi is pulling China back to Mao's personality worship and to Mao's oppression of the individual, Tsao asserts. "Xi Jinping doesn't care about human rights. He doesn't care about democracy. He wants to take over Taiwan. Xi doesn't care about what the local people want," Tsao declares. "One country, two systems," which is also the model for Hong Kong, Tsao describes as a propaganda tool to fool the last few gullible Taiwanese.

Tsao also believes that Xi doesn't care about the cost of trying to take Taiwan. "He's power-mad like Putin," he says, estimating that a Chinese takeover of Taiwan would be a step towards even more widespread Chinese power in the Pacific and open a path for China to world domination in the fight against the US. Therefore, Tsao wants to make sure that everyone realizes that it is nonsense when China says that China and Taiwan are the same nation. He vows to spend his remaining lifetime fighting for Taiwan.

After hearing from Robert Tsao, it is with great interest that I attend a Kuma Academy course on a Tuesday in January 2023.

It takes place in the parish hall—or more precisely the basement—of the Presbyterian Church. It's a full-day course with lessons on China's military, Chinese disinformation, especially on social media, first aid training, and how to protect yourself and your family as an internally displaced person. I have been provided a guest seat in the back. The course is otherwise overbooked. The participants are a mix of men and women and from all age groups.

The course starts out with the military situation in the Taiwan Strait. The teaching is practical. Participants are introduced to recognizing Chinese weapon systems by seeing photos of them on the screen. Just as the Ukrainian civilian population have been able to recognize and report Russian soldiers and weapons.

I also listen in on the course on Chinese disinformation. It includes examples from various social media. The teacher emphasizes that Chinese disinformation is used both before and during a war to break down the Taiwanese citizens' will to defend themselves. It's similar to war propaganda used in the past, but now combined with the possibilities of the internet. On the screen, the trainer shows various popular YouTube channels whose funding is under suspicion to be provided by the Chinese authorities to spread propaganda in Taiwan.

At one point, a photo of President Biden appears on the screen with a quote in Chinese. I instinctively think, before I read it, that the quote must be Biden's statement about his willingness to support Taiwan militarily. Wrong. It's a quote from Biden about Afghanistan from the 2021 withdrawal and the necessity of a people's willingness to defend themselves.

Interesting perspective, I think. The lesson from Afghanistan—also for Taiwan—is that there is only so much the US can do if the people themselves do not fight for their political system. Accordingly, Kuma Academy's mission is to instill a stronger will to defend themselves in the Taiwanese people.

I test this assumption during one of the breaks when I talk to a young woman and ask her why she is participating. She tells me that she wants to be able to contribute and to defend herself. She has taken a day off work to attend the course. The Ukrainians' willingness to defend their country has influenced her. She has often heard in the media that Taiwan is small and weak compared to China, but now she believes that Taiwan could be able to defend itself. I ask if she would also participate in military weapons training. She answers with both hands raised in a hand sign to show that she would not be able to lift a handheld rocket launcher or a similar weapon. She is a slender woman. She adds that the course gives her the belief that everyone—including her—can contribute to the defense of Taiwan in their own way.

I also talk to Kyle, a man in his forties, who states that "everyone should be able to contribute to the defense of Taiwan." He knows China well, having worked there for six years and encountered many different attitudes towards Taiwanese—including positive ones—among the Chinese. According to him, the problem is that the communist regime in Beijing is stuck in their negative attitude towards Taiwan as a free country.

While the participants are practicing first aid, I sit down with Marco Ho, CEO of Kuma Academy. He's wearing round glasses and a nice vest and tie. He has a history as a political candidate for a smaller and more pro-independence leaning party than the DPP.

Marco explains that Kuma means black bear in Taiwanese. It is a special variant of the bear that is only found in Taiwan. Therefore, the logo is a black bear holding a rifle, even though the academy does not offer weapons training. The bear is wearing a white V-collar—symbolizing the V in "victory".

The main purpose of the black bear training is to strengthen the defense will of the population and provide participants with hands-on training in civil defense techniques. Although Taiwan has been under threat for many years, it has been decades since there was last a conflict.

The ambition is to train three million Taiwanese citizens to become so-called black bears over the next three years. These are the years, when it really counts. Marco emphasizes that many say that Taiwan is particularly at risk of Chinese military provocations between now and 2027.

The donation from Robert Tsao has allowed Kuma Academy, which was formed in 2021, to develop rapidly. Kuma has expanded from a purely volunteer organization to a full-time staff by 2022 and to offer more courses.

I also ask about Ukraine and what observations Marco makes. "Ukraine's civil resistance is inspiring," he answers me. It shows that defending yourself is not only a military effort. It's also about being able to maintain a normal life and make society function as well as possible in a war situation. Marco cites as an example the joint effort to keep bakeries open in Ukraine so that people can get bread.

On the other hand, Ukraine is quite different from Taiwan, partly because Ukrainian displaced persons have been able to take up residence in other European countries. This possibility does not exist in Taiwan, where the sea is the neighboring country. This is why it is so important to train Taiwanese people to be internally displaced so that they can find the nearest shelter and other ways to protect themselves in a war situation. The same applies to the wounded, who must be transported to safety on local terms. This is where civilian first aid plays an important role.

I ask how Marco assesses the Taiwanese population's willingness to defend themselves. "Both high and great," is his assessment. He refers both to opinion polls that prove his point and to the influx of people attending Kuma Academy's courses, as well as the willingness of the people to make voluntary donations to their work. During Nancy Pelosi's visit, Kuma reached a peak of one million Taiwan dollars, or about 30,000 euros a day in individual contributions from ordinary citizens.

Although the people must be the backbone of self-defense, Marco emphasizes that it is important that other democratic countries support Taiwan as much as they can. Just as they have done in Ukraine.

When I return to the classroom, it's time for group work. Each group presents their "refugee backpack" and what they have packed for a crisis. Drinking water, snacks, sleeping bag, flashlight and Swiss Army knife are among the recurring items packed. However, one plans to bring some gold for payment. Another participant has added a pearl necklace to the list—it has personal significance, even in a crisis situation.

Prior to my trip to Taiwan, I discussed these civil society initiatives with Bonnie Glaser, one of the foremost American Taiwan experts and head of the Asia program at the German Marshall Fund think tank in Washington DC. She sees the initiatives as insufficient if civil and military defense are not better integrated: "It's not first aid that will stop China's missiles or military advance," she concludes. Bonnie Glaser is right that unless Taiwan's military is also ready for combat in the front line, civil defense power means less. That was also the lesson of Afghanistan's collapse in 2021.

But I do think that the importance of civil society initiatives should not be underestimated. In a democracy where the will of the people is the foundation, it is also the people's efforts that determine the will to defend. It is part of Taiwan's strength that civil society is so strong. This is precisely how a democratic system should mobilize against an authoritarian neighbor. I see first-hand in Taiwan, how participating in such courses can help boost motivation. It shifts the perspective from Taiwan being a small and underdog nation against China to how personal effort can make a difference to the future of their country.

CHAPTER 7

The global scramble for Taiwan's computer chips

Now we're moving down to the nanometer, a billionth of a meter. The naked eye can't assist us anymore. That's the size of semiconductors or computer chips. The basic component of computer chips are thin silicon wafers, and the chips are the building blocks of our modern world's technological computing power.

It is also over these miniature items that the power struggle between the US and China is being played out these years. Taiwan is in the middle.

There is only one place in the world where the smallest and most advanced computer chips are manufactured. It's in Taiwan. It produces around 60 percent of the world market for computer chips. If you prime the microscope down to three nanometers, Taiwanese engineers are global leaders in producing the world's smallest chips. They have a de facto global monopoly on the top-end of this technical skill.

The production of computer chips is referred to as Taiwan's silicon shield—a shield because it refers to the fact that Taiwan's key role in the production chain should secure the country against a devastating attack from China. Destroying chip production would bring the global economy—including

China's economy and technological supply chains—to a standstill.

The island and its electronics companies are an indispensable part of the world's globalized electronics supply chains. Computer chips are the oil of our time—also in geopolitical importance for the US and China and the rest of the world. Many ordinary people don't yet realize this.

What's more, it's one private Taiwanese company that towers above the others. Little known to the wider public, the company is hidden behind the four-letter acronym TSMC, Taiwan Semiconductor Manufacturing Company, founded in 1987 by engineer Morris Chang and originally supported by the Taiwanese government.

In terms of influence and size, it is the largest publicly traded company in Asia dwarfing Chinese and Japanese companies. This makes it one of the world's largest and most significant companies, but one that few have heard of.

However, Warren Buffett, the American investor guru, invested around five billion dollars in TSMC shares over the fall of 2022. Illustrating the newfound interest, the recent book *Chip War,* which chronicles the story of the semiconductor production and Taiwan's central role, has become a bestseller.

Our ubiquitous iPhones tell us that they are designed by Apple in California and assembled in China, but there is more to it: Taiwan. The real power ingredient that allows the phone to pack so much computing power into so little space is Taiwan's advanced microchips. Lots of microscopic chips go into an iPhone, especially from TSMC, which has enabled Apple to produce smaller and better over the last decade.

During the coronavirus pandemic, it was almost impossible to get a new car delivered quickly in most parts of the world. Waiting times can still be long. The reason is a shortage of computer chips in the supply chains. A new car can be fully constructed, but if even a single computer chip is missing, it won't drive anywhere. There are an estimated 1,500 chips in a regular car and up to twice as many in an electric car.

The need for chips is growing and is everywhere. It's not just in cars, iPhones, computers, Kindles that chips are indispensable. It's in our lawnmowers—unless you run a mechanical hand mower—hair dryers, hearing aids, digital watches, solar cells and heating systems in our homes. Take a look around you. You're surrounded by a world of microchips who power your everyday life and work.

THREE TRILLION GOOD REASONS TO AVOID A WAR WITH TAIWAN

In other words, Taiwan is the fulcrum of one of the most vital products in today's and tomorrow's market. And at the same time, Taiwan is in the middle of a conflict zone with China.

A military conflict—or even a blockade of Taiwan—would cause a severe slowdown in the global economy. Harder than Covid. Harder than Russia's war in Ukraine.

Even though Taiwan is much further away from us Europeans than Ukraine, a war there would have a much greater direct economic impact on our everyday lives. With conflict in the Taiwan Strait, we will not be able to get hold of electronic products and spare parts. All electronics prices would increase enormously.

War against Taiwan is an economic doomsday scenario. Both economists and national security experts have tried to calculate the bottom line in this scenario. According to Nikkei Asia, a Japanese media outlet, a Taiwan conflict would cause an immediate loss of around 2.6 trillion US dollars to the global economy. That's more than the total value of Italy—the EU's third-largest economy. Calculations by the research firm Rhodium Group, which purely analyzes the effects of a blockade of Taiwan, also end up at a figure over two trillion US dollars, in what the firm itself refers to as a conservative estimate.

The chip shield works precisely because the economic shock will also hit China, the likely aggressor. Taiwan's Minister of Economic Affairs Wang Mei-Hua summarized the scenario when she spoke in 2022 at a conference in Washington: "By interfering or disrupting Taiwan, China itself will also be greatly impacted." China is also dependent on Taiwanese chips in its supply chain—even if China can't buy the most advanced ones.

So there are trillions of good reasons not to start a conflict in the Taiwan Strait. As Minister of Economic Affairs Wang Mei-Hua frames it: "if Taiwan is safe, the global supply chain will also be secure." It is simply too expensive and thus too irrational to go to war over Taiwan.

But Putin's devastating war in Ukraine casts renewed doubt on whether Xi Jinping is listening to the sound economic reasons for staying on his side of the Taiwan Strait. Due to the uncertainty of China's war intentions, a larger geopolitical game is underway between the US and China. In the center, Taiwan's chip shield is being pressure tested.

USA, CHINA AND THE SUPERPOWER BATTLE FOR CHIPS

In the White House on August 9, 2022, President Joe Biden inked the US Chips and Science Act. It allocates 52 billion US dollars to rebuild the computer chip industry in the US. American engineers invented computer chips in the late 1950s. But since then, the US chip industry has declined from producing 30 percent to the current ten percent of global production.

For once, the two parties in Congress, the Democrats and the Republicans, were in lockstep on the passage of the Chip Act. The Act is about competition with China, and it promises new jobs in the US. The great power competition with China unites the otherwise divided American political spectrum.

During his years in the White House, Donald Trump tried to revitalize the American steel and coal industry. Now Biden is making the same attempt with computer chips. In the fall of 2022, the President travelled across the US with the message that the future of the chip is in the US.

Just after lunchtime on a warm November day in 2022 in California, Biden speaks to the employees of satellite company Viasat flashing his well-known big smile: "America invented these chips when we went to the Moon. America invented the computer chip… we led the industry for decades. But then something happened: America stopped investing in America."

Biden explains that the US can no longer rely on the global supply chain of computer chips. The 2021 automotive short-age during the pandemic showed how dependent that indus-try is on chips—and how dependent Americans are on being able to purchase new cars pronto. According to an article in the Wall Street Journal, it is estimated that the 2021 chip shortage cost the automotive industry over 210 billion US dollars.

Biden is determined to change that. In the future, the US should not be vulnerable to political decisions in China or Taiwan. Biden emphasizes that increased production in the US is a national security issue. Maintaining a world-class US military requires access to the best chips. " Guess what?" Biden rhetorically asks the ViaSat audience: "we were having trouble supplying the Javelin missiles to Ukraine because they didn't have the chips…To help defend themselves against Putin's brutal and unprovoked war", Biden emphasizes his point that the US must ensure sufficient production of computer chips on American soil. Otherwise, the US may lack the supplies to fight the wars of the future.

The American companies Intel and Micron, both of which are already in the chip business, have set aside extraordinarily large billion-dollar investments to follow up on the president's ambitions. In addition to the high-sounding words, it is of course also highly motivating for the two companies to gain access to government subsidies from the 52-billion-dollar appropriation.

When Biden speaks at Micron's announcement of their $100 billion investment in Syracuse, New York, he jokingly mentions that China's leader, Xi Jinping, is concerned. The audience laughs. " I'm not joking…as I told him, it's not about conflict, it's about competition. And we're back in the game. We're competing again in a big way."

China has joined the competition and allocated billions to become the leader in computer chips. China expectedly outspends the US and Europe. Funding is poured into Chinese state-owned companies that produce chips. China is well positioned when it comes to less advanced chips. Chinese scientists in the US—and Taiwanese scientists—are paid generous sums to locate their research in China. Behind closed doors, China's industrial spies are working across the globe—including in Taiwan—to intercept production secrets that could push China one or more nanometers further ahead in the chip race.

On October 7, 2022, the Biden administration took aim at China in their chip competition, introducing new US regulations. They restrict China's access to advanced chips. It is therefore a tough blow to China's ambitions to become the leading military power and tech nation over the coming decades.

Even though the US itself has lost ground in the global race to be the leader in computer chips, the administration can still enforce restrictions against China globally. This is due to the inclusion of US components or patents that are used throughout the supply chain. The new US rules make such components illegal to sell to China—even for third parties such as European and Taiwanese companies. In this way, the US restrictions place a powerful brake on the global supply chain to China—even for Taiwanese companies that continue to sell chips—though never the most advanced ones—to the Chinese market.

As Biden's security advisor Jake Sullivan emphasizes in connection with the launch of the restrictions, they are not intended to hit China's economic development, but solely to prevent China's military access to advanced chips. Until now, China's military has used market access to the civilian global market for chips to try to get ahead in the race to introduce artificial intelligence in weapons production. Already, China is a global leader in several types of drones.

In relation to China, the US can try to limit access to chips, but if the US itself is to return to the top league of chip production, it requires the Taiwanese companies and especially TSMC to be on board.

That's why Morris Chang, the iconic nonagenarian founder of TSMC, is seen in Arizona on December 7, 2022, as TSMC opens a chip factory in Phoenix, a total investment of 40 billion US dollars. The factories will produce chips down to 4 and 3 nanometers by 2026. This makes TSMC the largest foreign investor ever in Arizona, and hundreds of skilled Taiwanese engineers have moved to the desert state. No one else has the technical know-how to produce the chips. But thousands of local jobs are also created. The investment decision has been in the works at TSMC for a while, but the decision was accelerated and billions more were thrown in when TSMC's management sensed the new political winds in the US.

Both Joe Biden and Apple CEO Tim Cook are on stage for the opening. In the background is a CAT truck adorned with a giant American flag. It frames the mixed motives for getting Taiwan to relocate production to the US. There is a clear security dimension, because production in the US cannot be jeopardized by a Chinese attack on Taiwan. In addition, there is trade nationalism. The shift is illustrated by the fact that Tim Cook, a former defender of borderless trade globalization and production in China, happily declares on stage that Apple's chips can now be stamped "made in America".

Morris Chang, who began his career in computer chips in the US at Texas Instruments in the 1950s, also speaks at the launch, expressing his pride in TSMC's investment, but also delivering a nostalgic observation that both globalization and free trade as we used to know it are bygone in the world, in which we now live in.

Manufacturing in the US pokes holes in Taiwan's chip shield as the importance of Taiwan as a chip manufacturing country diminishes by moving overseas.

But from what I hear, TSMC, and thus Taiwan, still has an edge in that development. The so-called "holy grail" will remain in Taiwan as a security and commercial shield. This means that chip production in the US will only go down to three nanometers and only after a few years. Research and experimental production in two or one nanometer take place under top secret and protected conditions in Taiwan.

CHIPS FOR EUROPE?

The EU—led by French Industry Commissioner Thierry Breton—has also launched a chip law. It has considerably less funding than the US and China, but equal in ambition to boost research and chip production. The German and French automotive industries also experienced the weaknesses in chip supply chains during the coronavirus pandemic. "Europe cannot and will not lag behind," Breton writes on Linkedin, and continues that "With the European Chips Act, our tech sovereignty is within reach." Breton has the same ambition as Biden. Chips must be produced in Europe to make the continent resilient to conflicts between the US, China and Taiwan.

The EU would also like Taiwanese companies to set up in Europe, but Europe does not have the same security attractiveness as the US. The US under Biden is unequivocally ready to defend Taiwan—and its chip production—against an attack from China.

As one Taiwanese expert diplomatically put it to me: "Europe needs some really good other incentives." He's thinking of money, i.e. government subsidies, and that materializes when the EU and the German government co-sponsor a TSMC investment in Dresden with total investments over 10 billion euros.

Clear value politics and support for Taiwan can also play a positive role when it comes to computer chips. In December 2020, Prime Minister Kotryna Simonyté and Foreign Minister Gabrielius Landsbergis took office in Vilnius, the capital of Lithuania. Both are champions of a global, values-based policy that supports democracy and freedom globally—including when it comes to Taiwan. This came to fruition the following year.

I was in Vilnius at the end of 2021, where a new Taiwan office was opened. Typically, in order not to offend China, such representative offices are labelled "Taipei", but the Lithuanians went a step further and allowed Taiwan in the name. China's government was furious. They saw the office's name as a violation of the One China policy and launched an economic and diplomatic crackdown. Lithuania was temporarily removed as an independent country from China's customs list. In practice, trade stopped almost completely.

But all was not doom and gloom financially for Lithuania, as the Taiwanese government simultaneously stepped up with ten million euros for a fund to increase cooperation with Lithuania on Taiwan's chip production.

Similarly, Taiwan has initiated small-scale computer chip collaborations with Slovakia and the Czech Republic—both countries that have been vocal in their support for Taiwan.

There is also another link to Europe in the global chip food chain. Dutch company ASML produces highly specialized lithography machines that are indispensable for chip manufacturing. ASML sells machines to TSMC, which makes the chips for Apple products. But ASML also sells to China—or did. In 2023, the US government worked hard and successfully to get NATO ally, the Netherlands to halt ASML's sales to China. Of course, dropping the Chinese market is a financial loss for ASML and the Netherlands. But here, security policy and relations with the US trump economic considerations.

PIONEERS IN TAIWAN'S CHIP INDUSTRY

While in Taiwan, I meet with a few founders from the chip industry and I visit Hsinchu, the Taiwanese city where computer chip production started and remains the city's backbone.

In Taipei, I speak with Robert Tsao, the founder of UMC, which was founded in 1980, seven years before TSMC, but is now the second largest company after TSMC. Readers have already been acquainted with Tsao in the previous chapter on Taiwan's private civil defense.

Robert Tsao and I also talk about Taiwan's chip manufacturing, which is a significant part of Tsao's career. In the early 1970s, he graduated from Taiwan National University, a prestigious school, as an engineer specializing in electricity. A job at a government research company later followed, where Robert's talent was discovered and he got an opportunity to travel to the US to learn about chip production.

The then forward-thinking Taiwanese Minister of Industry K.T. Li saw an opportunity to position Taiwan in chip production and create jobs on the island. Maybe he was so foresighted that he thought of national security too and that Taiwanese chip production could become a chip shield. At least, the timing coincides with the Republic of China/Taiwan losing US diplomatic recognition and security guarantees in 1979, and Taiwan establishing its first computer chip company, UMC—United Microelectronics Corporation, in 1980.

On Wikipedia and other web-sources, Robert Tsao is referred to as the founder of the UMC, but when I highlight that achievement in our conversation, he argues that it is more accurate to say that the Taiwanese state was the real founder. The government provided the initial capital, he explains. However, he adds modestly that as head of UMC, he contributed to making the company profitable. That is still the case. According to Forbes' global ranking, UMC is now bigger than large Danish companies like Carlsberg and Vestas.

Tsao also highlights that he introduced an employee share program where employees were paid shares instead of salary.

This gave employees the motivation to fight for the company. The share program also made it possible to recruit the best Taiwanese engineers, especially those working in the US.

Among the returning engineers from the US was a certain Morris Chang. He had worked in the US since the 1950s for Texas Instruments, while the first computer chips were invented by American scientists.

Then in 1987, Morris Chang founded TSMC in Taiwan with the active support of the Taiwanese government. The company grew much larger than UMC and any other company in the world in its field. Throughout the 1980s, the main competitor was Japan and Japanese companies, but TSMC steadily increased its market share. Samsung in South Korea, however, remains a major player and competitor.

Robert Tsao describes himself as the co-inventor of the business success of the Taiwanese chip model. It is the same model behind both UMC and TSMC.

The genius of Taiwan was to focus solely on chip manufacturing and become the world's best and most accurate at it. Before Taiwanese companies got into manufacturing from the 1980s onwards, the business model of American companies had been to design, produce and sell chips.

This is still the division of labor for TSMC today, with major customer Apple designing the chips and TSMC producing them. UMC supplies chips to the automotive industry. Another player is Taiwanese chip manufacturer Macronix, which supplies the chips inside Nintendo products. The Taiwanese companies are globally unknown company names, but they provide the indispensable components for an iPhone, car or a Nintendo Switch or Game Boy.

Looking back, Robert Tsao calls it "the wildest dream" that the industry has grown so big in Taiwan. The city of Hsinchu is Taiwan's answer to Silicon Valley, located on the coast of the Taiwan Strait south of the capital Taipei. It was a government initiative to offer industry land there.

MY VISIT TO HSINCHU—THE CHIP CITY

The high-speed train journey from Taipei to Hsinchu takes me only half an hour in January 2023. In 1980, Hsinchu was without a fast connection to the capital.

I've arranged a meeting with the CEO and founder of Macronix, Wu Miin, who in 1989 successfully returned from studying at Stanford University and subsequently worked at Intel in Silicon Valley. He and his company have been based in Hsinchu ever since.

In true Danish style, I arrive at Macronix's massive headquarters on a city bike, which Wu Miin and the staff find both surprising and entertaining. I'm escorted to the top floor—the executive floor—with a beautiful sun-drenched view of the lush green mountains that dominate the eastern side of Taiwan.

Wu Miin has a twinkle in his eye and a funny way of telling his own self-made entrepreneurial story. Unlike Robert Tsao and Morris Chang, Wu Miin hasn't had the government behind him, just his own ingenuity. His company and fortune are built on spotting a market opening.

When Japan opened its manufacturing to foreign companies in the late 1980s as part of a trade agreement with the US, it also made room for an enterprising start-up like Macronix, which became a subcontractor of chips to Nintendo. In this way, Wu Miin creates the start-up capital that is a prerequisite for large-scale production in the chip industry.

He says that another success parameter is that he managed to lure other Taiwanese engineers back from the US—a so-called reverse brain-drain. These achievements have earned Wu Miin a spot on the cover of Forbes magazine—the issue is proudly displayed and hangs in a glass and frame on the wall.

Wu Miin is also a good diplomat, so he deftly avoids answering my geopolitical questions about the US and China. The same applies to Taiwanese politics. On the walls, I spot, company photos of visits from both the DPP and KMT governments over the past decades. It's politically savvy. Most Taiwanese businesspeople want to make money—shielded from politics and geopolitical headwinds.

However, Wu Miin does deliver a few political assessments. We're talking about Huawei, which Macronix previously had as a customer until US sanctions made it impossible. Wu Miin refers to Huawei's founder, Ren Zhengfei, as entrepreneurial and someone who knows how to "motivate employees" and make "things succeed". Miin believes that Huawei—even with US restrictions—can help drive China's technological prowess forward. Later in the fall of 2023, Chinese technology and phone-maker Huawei demonstrates capacity by introducing a 7-nanometer indigenous chip, accelerating the chips race.

Wu Miin doesn't like the chip shield metaphor when I mention it. In his view, talking about a shield could increase the risk of war. "It's all about grabbing the shield," and that creates conflict, he observes. He is clearly concerned that China could increase the potential for conflict with Taiwan if it feels technologically restrained by the US.

I ask about his assessment of the US's increasing restrictions on the export of advanced chips to China. Wu Miin believes that this will limit China's development in the short term. He has no doubt that China is going to waste a lot of money in government subsidies handed out blindly to build a globally leading chip industry. But in the longer term, "who knows?" he says, pointing to Taiwan's own venture into computer chips, which also succeeded. "We'll see in 20 years," he concludes.

As I cycle from the Macronix headquarters back to the train station, I notice that Hsinchu is now home to some of the most expensive real estate neighborhoods in the country. The chip industry has grown large and profitable. It's the Silicon Valley of Taiwan.

NEW HOLES IN TAIWAN'S CHIP SHIELD?

The rise of computer chip production in Taiwan is also part of the success of economic globalization that we have been accustomed to since the fall of the Berlin Wall and the entry of China into the world economy. Production has located itself wherever it was most convenient and cheapest. Consumers around the world have benefited from ever cheaper and better technological products. No one gave much thought to the fact that supply chains were built directly across a 70-year-old conflict line between China and Taiwan.

That era is ending these years. Morris Chang, TSMC's founder, has good reason to be nostalgic about globalization. The chip industry is now unambiguously security policy. In my view, this presents three risks for Taiwan's chip shield.

The first comes from China, whose leadership is naturally angry at being shut out of the global technological food chain of advanced chips by the US, partly supported by Taiwan and its companies. This could lead to one nightmare scenario— which is also being discussed in Washington—where China sees an interest in taking over Taiwan to capture their chip production as well. An American security pundit, Elbridge

Colby, argues that Taiwan must promise to destroy semiconductor facilities if China invades to ensure that China cannot take over production. Another equally nightmarish option is that China would target Taiwan's production capacity. The perverse logics would be that if China can't enjoy the chips, neither can the rest of the world.

However, it remains true that China will also suffer economically, but the logic could be that the others, i.e. the US and Western countries, will suffer even more if the world lacks advanced chips. China is in a good position when it comes to less advanced chips for cars and many other products that are manufactured large-scale in China. It contains a similar twisted logic to Putin, who bets that he can turn the tide of war in Ukraine because democratic governments cannot keep their "as long as it takes" promise to Ukraine due to election cycles and "war fatigue".

The second danger is the regionalization of Taiwan's chip production and in particular TSMC to the US, Europe and Japan. The US is putting political pressure and giving economic incentives to Taiwanese companies to relocate production to the US, protected from a Chinese attack.

If global manufacturing of chips moves out from Taiwan, holes will appear in Taiwan's chip shield. Cynically, this shift in production could well make a future US administration much less willing to defend Taiwan militarily. Presidential Republican candidate Vivek Ramaswamy has voiced such opinions.

The third danger is technological. Can Taiwan remain at the top of the chip innovation food chain? The chip industry and computer revolution has been based on Gordon Moore's Law from 1965. It states that the capacity of computer chips doubles every 18 months. This prediction has held true for decades, as chips have been made smaller and better. But as chips get down to one nanometer, a natural point is likely to occur where even Taiwan's world-class engineers can't keep building smaller and more powerful chips. Innovation might arise from another technology beyond making chips smaller.

CHAPTER 8

Taiwan's economic resilience against China

It's not just through computer chips that China and Taiwan are economically connected to each other and to the world market.

With its 1.4 billion inhabitants, China is a huge market. The world's second largest economy with 18 trillion US dollars compared to the US' 23 trillion. There has been high growth for as long as many of us can remember. Since China's entry into the World Trade Organization in 2001, China's role and size in world markets has skyrocketed. China is an economic magnet.

Also for Taiwan, enjoying a solid trade surplus with China. Taiwan's economy is about 23 times smaller than China's, but Taiwan is almost twice the size of the Danish economy.

China is by far Taiwan's largest trading partner, even though the Taiwanese government under President Tsai Ing-wen has spearheaded efforts for new markets for Taiwanese companies beyond China.

As part of China's toolbox, the Middle Kingdom uses its state control of the economy to provide both carrots and sticks to Taiwan. Economic carrots for Taiwanese businesspeople and politicians who speak up for China in Taiwan. Sticks for independence-seeking politicians and their voters. I witness both tools in play by China on Kinmen, the island close to mainland China.

Chinese government economic blackmail is not limited to Taiwan. China is increasingly using the same methods against other countries and individual companies until they toe Beijing's line. Often, the mere threat of being shut out of China's market is effective.

While Chinese and Taiwanese jet fighters duel in the Taiwan Strait, supply chains still flow effortlessly between China and Taiwan.

The goods flowing back and forth are, of course, computer chips and a wide range of other electronic products. Taiwan is responsible for the more sophisticated part of the electronics. Chinese factories—also owned by Taiwanese companies like Foxconn—add smaller parts, package and prepare for sale. The supply chain goes from Taiwan to China and on to us consumers in the US and Europe.

Several Taiwanese analysts mention Foxconn and its electronics factories in China as the best—or worst, depending on your political persuasion—example when I talk to them about integration with China. Foxconn is estimated to be China's largest private employer, with employees in China numbering not in the thousands, but closer to a million. However, Foxconn is in the process of moving production to India and Vietnam.

The Foxconn factories produce for Apple, Samsung and Sony and are the world's largest technology contract manufacturer. In 2022, the company's annual revenue reached 213 billion US dollars and was ranked 20th in the 2023 Fortune Global 500.

In 2022, Taiwan exported 40,7 percent to China, including Hong Kong, according to government statistics. Taiwanese exports to the US, on the other hand, are at 14,8 percent. The trade figures reflect a reverse security policy situation, where Taiwan relies on the US for protection from China. This makes Taiwan quite closely linked or, as some might put it, economically dependent on China. From the Chinese side, it has been a deliberate policy to promote economic integration with Taiwan. This is a way of forging an inextricable link between China and Taiwan. It is part of the Communist Party's peaceful means of securing unification with Taiwan.

IS TAIWAN'S CHINA TRADE TOO MUCH OF A GOOD THING?

Trade with China divides politicians and people in Taiwan. The Nationalist Party wants closer economic cooperation with the mainland, while the Democratic Progressive Party stands for anything-but-China.

From 2008 to 2016, under President Ma Ying-jeou of the Nationalist Party, more than 20 economic agreements were signed between China and Taiwan. The agreements opened the two economies to each other in both air and sea travel and labor exchange. Chinese tourists also flocked to Taiwan in droves—or more accurately, in the millions.

Taiwanese moved to China in large numbers also for new economic opportunities. In 2015, during Ma Ying-jeou's last year in office, around 420,000 Taiwanese worked in China. By the end of 2020, the number had dropped to 242,000 according to a Globe and Mail report, probably due to a worsening political climate between Taiwan and China and, of course, the corona travel restrictions.

However, Ma Ying-jeou's economic rapprochement policy with China ended up encountering popular resistance in Taiwan, culminating in the Sunflower Revolution in 2014. In 2013, the Ma government had signed another economic agreement with China in the banking, healthcare and film industries, among others. The agreement just needed to be passed in parliament, where the Nationalist Party held the majority. In March 2014, angry students occupied the parliament building, initially demanding a public debate on the agreement and subsequently that the agreement be scrapped.

The sunflower became the common symbol of the protesters as a local florist handed out sunflowers outside the occupied parliament.

There are many twists and turns to the story, but the short conclusion was that the Sunflower occupiers won. The agreement with China was never ratified by parliament, despite the Nationalist Party's majority. The occupiers cleaned up nicely after themselves as they left the parliament building where they had been living for over a month.

The Sunflower Revolution remains for many an important marker in Taiwan's democratic development. Several of the protesters continued their activism in one way or another. One is now in the government—Digital Minister Audrey Tang. And in parliament is independent heavy metal singer Freddy Lim. Several others I meet in Taiwan refer to the Sunflower Revolution as a marker event in their lives.

The popular sentiment against further economic cooperation with China was also an important factor when Tsai Ing-wen of the DPP was elected president in 2016. The chill then went both ways. China shut down dialogue and further economic agreements as Tsai, in China's reading, does not recognize the one-China policy and the 1992 Consensus, which is China's basic line for contacts.

Tsai's government has sought to find new trading partners instead of China. Under her, the Taiwanese government has also tightened regulations to make Chinese acquisitions of Taiwanese companies more difficult, especially in sensitive sectors from computer chips to solar cells. Similarly, the Taiwanese government under Tsai is much more vigilant about Taiwanese companies moving their technology to China.

Foxconn has been fined by the Taiwanese government for entering a computer chip collaboration with a Chinese company without government permission. Foxconn's Taiwanese owner, Terry Gou, is not only a billionaire but also a political player who tried to run as KMT and independent candidate for President before he dropped out of the race in late November 2023. Perhaps also due to his own business interests in China, he has been highly critical of President Tsai and the lack of dialogue with Beijing.

For the DPP government, it's all about finding new markets beyond China. That's why, when I discuss Taiwan's trade policy with Foreign Minister Wu, he also highlights the "southbound policy" as one of the government's priority areas. Under this policy, the government is doing what it can to encourage Taiwanese companies to open their eyes to trade opportunities in Southeast Asian countries such as Vietnam, Malaysia and Singapore—often abbreviated to ASEAN countries named after the regional cooperation organization. Trade with these countries has increased, reaching 14,8 percent in 2022 according to official figures. This puts the overall percentage slightly above the US.

The trade figures shows that the Tsai government has not succeeded in substantially reducing trade with China or diversifying to ASEAN. Eight years of the DPP in power has not altered the fundamental magnetic force of the Chinese market.

TAIWAN'S DIFFICULT SEARCH FOR NEW MARKETS AND OPPORTUNITIES

There are good reasons for that. It's not easy for Taiwan to enter new markets. China's economic anaconda strategy is working. It involves China squeezing Taiwan in its grip while preventing other countries from expanding cooperation.

Still, Taiwan has a presence on the world trade map. Albeit under the name Chinese Taipei, but as an independent member of the World Trade Organization (WTO). This membership became possible as part of a US-led compromise from 2001, where a then economically and politically weaker China was also admitted to the organization and had to accept that Taiwan, as an independent customs territory, was also admitted.

Today, China is much stronger and uses its economic and diplomatic muscle to intimidate other countries from entering into economic agreements with Taiwan. In recent times, Taiwan has only managed to conclude free trade agreements with two smaller markets such as Singapore and New Zealand.

Taiwan has also been excluded from multilateral free trade agreements in Asia because China plays such a large role in the economies of other countries. These countries do not want to risk their trade relationship with China by entering into trade agreements with Taiwan. Also in the economic field, it is Goliath versus David.

The EU and member states like Denmark also dare not enter into economic agreements with Taiwan for fear of China.

Since Denmark signed a double taxation agreement with Taiwan in 2006, no other bilateral agreements have been signed.

In the European Parliament, however, there is a widespread desire among parliamentarians to conclude an investment agreement with Taiwan that can strengthen economic cooperation. Yet the European Commission has not even presented a draft for negotiations. At the end of 2020, under the German Presidency and the leadership of Chancellor Angela Merkel, an investment agreement with China was agreed. However, in 2021, China's Ministry of Foreign Affairs issued sanctions against European Members of Parliament—and my workplace, the Alliance of Democracies Foundation—in response to the EU sanctioning Chinese officials for human rights violations in Xinjiang, sparking outrage. The European Parliament has managed to put the adoption of the China investment agreement on complete hold, but without being able to turn the ship around and negotiate an agreement with Taiwan instead.

The US has also realized that Taiwan needs different economic opportunities to China. Clearly, Taiwan is vulnerable to China in the economic sphere. But since 2016 and Trump's time in power, the US has stopped making tariff-reducing free trade agreements that need approval from Congress. Trump started his term in 2017 by tearing up the free trade agreement (TPP) with Asia that Obama had signed. The same skepticism exists in Congress, where such free trade agreements must be passed.

However, the US administration has taken a smaller trade initiative with Taiwan. In June 2022, the US and Taiwan began negotiations on a 21st century agreement—the US-Taiwan Initiative on 21st-Century Trade—and in May 2023, a partial agreement was reached. The intention is to strengthen trade and economic cooperation. But while the US and Taiwan are drafting trade policy statements, China trade continues even without political support.

CHINA'S TRADE AND ECONOMIC COERCION

China uses its vast domestic market for more than benign trade cooperation. It's also seeking to make countries, companies and individuals follow the messages from the Communist Party's headquarters in Beijing, especially when it comes to Taiwan.

Even with the economic reform policies in China that allowed for private economic initiative, the Communist Party has never fully let go of the reins. Although they introduced some market economy, the party still directs the country's economy, including businesses and citizens, in an authoritarian way that free countries are unable to do.

In Denmark, we experienced such a Chinese reaction back in 2009, when then Prime Minister Lars Løkke Rasmussen received the Dalai Lama, Tibetan spiritual leader and Nobel Prize winner, at the official residence Marienborg. China, however, sees the Dalai Lama as a dangerous separatist working for Tibetan independence. I can be spotted as an official in the background in press photos from the Marienborg visit. As penance for the sin that the visit represented against the Communist Party, the Danish government shortly afterwards signed a note verbale, a diplomatic declaration, which stated that Denmark would oppose Tibetan independence. Previously, Danish policy was to work for Tibetan cultural autonomy within the Chinese constitution. That policy disappeared. The note was obviously dictated from Beijing. The fear of greater trade reprisals alone drove the Danish government to kowtow to China. We curtailed our right for a prime minister to meet with whomever he wants in his own country. China's tactics worked. No Danish prime minister has since met with the Dalai Lama.

In recent years, China has increased both the frequency and intensity of its economic coercion. They have been relatively successful. Governments like Denmark's have accommodated China in one way or another. But there are also countries that are standing up to the trade bully.

In 2020, Australia faced a series of trade restrictions in the Chinese market on Australian wine, lobsters, wheat and coal. China's representative in Australia submitted a 14-point list of complaints for Australia to rectify for China to normalize trade relations. One point to address was Australia's "reckless interference" in Taiwan, among others.

Fortunately, the Australian government has had steel in its backbone and hasn't signed any verbal notes nor apologized. As former Australian Prime Minister Malcolm Turnbull highlights in a public talk with the Alliance of Democracies Foundation, the lesson is never to bow to bully tactics. Instead, Australian producers sought new markets. Especially for its wine producers. Before the restrictions, China was by far the largest market for Australian wine. Expectedly, winemakers will never return to the Chinese market to the same extent, given the political risk.

Another clash regarding Taiwan, as I have already mentioned, took place in the Baltics. China restricted almost all trade with Lithuania after it opened a Taiwan representative office in Vilnius in November 2021. In Vilnius, the government is not bowing to Chinese economic pressure either. Initially, this led to economic losses for Lithuanian companies, but I'm told by now former Lithuanian Deputy Foreign Minister Mantas Adomenas, a chief architect behind the rapprochement with Taiwan, that after just one year, the Lithuanian economy has diversified from the loss from China. Instead of China, Lithuania has put political priority on opening new markets among democratic countries in Asia such as South Korea, Australia and Taiwan. Both the US and EU also helped with short-term relief and export facilitation.

Companies can also be pressured by China. Some years ago, the Marriott hotel chain was threatened by China with restrictions on access to the Chinese market, where Marriott has many hotels. This was because an American employee at a Marriott hotel in the US had listed Taiwan as an independent country in a guest questionnaire. Marriott took corrective action, even by laying off the employee. It became an ominous example of how an authoritarian country's standards can set the bar for workers' rights, even inside a free country like the United States.

The Chinese government also launched a campaign of threats against international airlines to change their flight maps so that Taiwan no longer appeared as an independent country and travel destination. The US government opposed China's actions and supported the free right of US airlines to list Taiwan as they wanted to, but China's threats worked because access to its aviation market is so important. China won a victory through its economic bullying muscle.

CHINA'S ECONOMIC PRESSURE ON TAIWAN

What do pineapple, fish and Taiwan beer have to do with each other? They are all three products from Taiwan, which China has banned from its market.

In the years with Tsai Ing-wen and the DPP in power, China has shifted from economic enticements to applying strategic pressure on Taiwan's economy and political life.

Whenever China is unhappy with political decisions in Taiwan, Taiwanese goods are banned from China. This happened during Nancy Pelosi's visit in August 2022, when frozen fish and other Taiwanese goods were banned.

I witness economic coercion at play myself in December 2022 while in Taiwan. Taiwan Beer, a local beer brand, gets banned in China. A social media campaign spontaneously emerges under the hashtag #FreedomBeer, where people show their support by buying and drinking the Taiwanese beer. A similar social media phenomenon occurred with the China-boycotted Australian wine with #FreedomWine. These movements are a new form of consumer activism.

I ask Foreign Minister Joseph Wu why China penalizes Taiwanese products and how effective that is. "Economic coercion serves two purposes" he explains. First, it's to scare Taiwanese voters by showing that China can directly target such economic coercion.

Secondly, it is a political signal to Taiwanese voters that China's economic pressure will continue so long as the DPP remains in power. In doing so, China is trying to tip the political balance in Taiwan and show that the Nationalist Party, the current opposition party, is a better alternative for the economic well-being of individual Taiwanese citizens.

Wu adds that some products are selected for their political and electoral potential. One example is a Chinese ban on pineapple, which is primarily produced in Southern Taiwan among DPP core voters. In this way, China is signaling that their Taiwanese independence leanings are hurting their economic bottom line.

In early January 2023, I visited the island of Kinmen, which is very close to mainland China. It is also a microcosm of China's economic inducements and coercion.

Shortly before I arrive on the island, China had imposed a product ban on "gaoliang", a local strong schnapps. The factory, owned by the local government, is important to the economy. The island's economy, which primarily depends on trade with China, has already been hit hard by the COVID-19 lockdown in China and the closure of ferry services to China.

I meet with Kinmen's only representative in Taiwan's parliament, Chen Yu-Jen, a no-nonsense woman in her forties, to understand her perspectives on the local economy and the relationship with China. She represents the Nationalist Party, which is much stronger locally on the island than the DPP, which has only in recent years established a smaller local base and secured political candidates. Chen Yu-Jen has studied in both the US and China, so she has personal knowledge of the two major powers that determine the fate of Taiwan.

She asks me if I know how many ferries normally run between Kinmen and the Chinese city of Xiamen? "Not exactly," I admit. "44 every single day, so it's a shuttle service. With up to 200–300 passengers, that's thousands of people traveling back and forth," she elaborates. Those ferries are economic lifelines. That's why Chen is also working hard to get the ferry connections to China back on track.

Actually, all political forces on the island agree that economic relations with China must be re-established. This includes the local DPP county councilor, Tsai Chi-yung, with whom I have lunch in his village, where almost all inhabitants carry the surname Tsai, as they have done for hundreds of years. In his office, Tsai shows me a photo of President Tsai Ing-wen on visit. One of her distant Tsai ancestors also originated from the village. But the county councillor differs significantly from the party line of the DPP in Taipei on economic ties with China. Like his local KMT opponent, Tsai supports economic cooperation with China. There are few other alternatives when you are located two kilometers from the Chinese city of Xiamen with its shopping and economic opportunities.

In response to the China ban on gaoliang, MP Chen tells me that she has already visited Xiamen in China to negotiate a solution. She hasn't succeeded yet, but she also plans to go to Beijing and negotiate further. This is a big difference from Taiwan's central government, which currently has only intermittent contacts and no real negotiations with China. Chen works for local interests—and in that regard, China appears to be the economic solution.

I ask Chen if she's worried about that by negotiating, she's endorsing China's economic coercion, but she insists that her constituents among Kinmen citizens don't see it that way. "Locally, they can work with China. The economic and human relations are characterized by being very close."

For a long time, China has also used economic incentives to bring China closer to mainland China. This goes back a long way. In fact, already when Xi Jinping, on his way to power, was governor of Fujian province in 1999–2002. In that function, he was instrumental in pushing for closer ties with China. He proposed that water, electricity and gas be supplied to Kinmen from the mainland. In addition, a bridge should be built from the mainland to Kinmen. Cooperation opportunities that Xi Jinping has reiterated as supreme leader in a speech in 2019.

Chen explains to me that the water supply was established in 2018. Now the citizens of China are drinking water from

China. The Taiwanese government was skeptical but ended up not opposing the move. Chen would like to take that forward and receive electricity and gas from China. It is expensive for Kinmen to get energy from Taiwan, she explains. However, she adds that it is hard to imagine that the current government in Taipei would accept such increased cooperation with China. I understand that reasoning, considering our negative European experience with Russian gas pipelines.

Kinmen's shared history with mainland China is complex. The island is the only part of Taiwan that has fought militarily against mainland-China back in 1949, 1954 and 1958. As a result, the island is full of military memorials and riddled like Swiss cheese with defense tunnels, now mostly walked by tourists from China as well. Kinmen's civilian population was subjected to constant artillery fire from Mao's soldiers on the mainland for a prolonged period in 1958. Chen tells me that several of her grandmother's siblings died. Chen explains that this is why the Kinmen Islanders are so determined that they want peace. It's a lesson from their bloody history.

According to her, the increased tension in the Taiwan Strait is all about China and the US fighting to be the strongest in the world. China and Taiwan risk becoming a battleground for the superpowers. And according to Chen, the citizens of Kinmen don't care who is the boss of the world.

I ask Chen what freedom means to the citizens of China and what it means to be part of Taiwan's democracy. "We value it, of course," she says. "But you don't have to rub China's nose in it." Chen highlights the period under KMT President Ma as a good period where the right balance between Taiwan and China was hit.

So how does Chen see China's long-term strategy to incorporate Taiwan and Kinmen into China, I continue my questioning. Chen's strategy is for Taiwan to maintain communication with China. "We've kept the peace for 70 years. Let's try for another 70 years," she replies. It is important to ensure that the Taiwan issue does not push itself to the top of the Chinese leadership's agenda. Chen believes this can be achieved by keeping communication with Beijing always open.

A final quirky anecdote illustrates the complexity of Kinmen and China's economic pressure policy. During my visit, a Brian Hioe, a Taiwanese-based journalist brings a news story to my attention. It tells the story of Australian lobsters—which are on the list of China's banned goods—are being smuggled into the Chinese market through Kinmen and labeled as a local product. The Chinese customs authorities hadn't spotted that the lobsters originate from sanctioned Australia.

Kudos to the Kinmen smugglers for local creativity to eke out a living while trying to navigate a geopolitically complicated world. I also hope that Kinmen find buyers for their local brandy gaoliang—preferably somewhere other than the Chinese market, so I pass on the recommendation. It is strong stuff, I can vouch for that after toasting it with Councillor Tsai.

IS TAIWAN'S CHINA TRADE A SECURITY POLICY ACHILLES HEEL?

Even with active efforts by the Taiwanese government to find new markets to reduce dependence on China, they have not fundamentally succeeded.

The US has also discovered relatively late that the defense of Taiwan is not only military, but also economic. In Europe, we remain too afraid of China to strengthen trade cooperation with Taiwan, except for a few brave Eastern European countries.

So, is it the economy that is Taiwan's real Achilles heel against China? This view is presented to me from an unexpected angle, namely from former Admiral Richard Chen, with whom I discuss military scenarios in Chapter 5. "We are making a lot of money," Richard Chen emphasizes. He refers to Taiwan's trade surplus with China, which in 2022 is around 110 billion US dollars.

"Can we change Taiwan's business model or find an alternative market?" Chen asks rhetorically, answering his own question with an "absolutely not". For Chen, Taiwan's trade surplus with China is therefore the real security threat. There is no other country, including the US, that would be able to quickly replace China economically and receive Taiwan's surplus exports.

The need for a complete alternative market would only arise if China took its economic pressure policy to the extreme and cut Taiwan fully off economically.

Of course, such an economic blockade would also affect China's own economy, but its economy is many times larger than Taiwan's and rivals the US in size. Interestingly, the military analyst and former Commander Chen singles out the economy as Taiwan's security weakness.

CHAPTER 9

Taiwan's digital resilience against China

"It's a textbook example of disinformation," observes Audrey Tang, Taiwan's digitization minister, when we meet. She refers to the Kansai disinformation case. Kansai is the airport at Osaka in Japan, where a typhoon hit in September 2018. Chaos ensued. Everyone tried to be flown home to safety—including several hundred Taiwanese and Chinese tourists.

Among the distressed Taiwanese and their families, a news story spread on social media and through chat groups that China's authorities provide better conditions and faster evacuation than Taiwan's. Such better conditions could also benefit Taiwanese, if they identified themselves as Chinese. The discrimination caused angry emojis to flare up on Taiwanese social media. The critical comments rained down on the Taiwanese consulate in Osaka. Why did the staff provide worse assistance than China?

There's one problem with the story. It is a false story—or in modern English "fake news". It is not based on facts, as the non-governmental organization Taiwan FactCheck Center later concluded. It is a civil society organization which works to uncover misinformation and disinformation. The story turns out to have been planted by Chinese sources to trigger strong emotions among Taiwanese citizens on social media. The events lead to tragic consequences. A Taiwanese consulate employee commits suicide, leaving a note that he feels that he failed the Taiwanese citizens in their time of need. A hoax on the Internet ended in a deadly outcome.

CHINESE PSYCHOLOGICAL AND DIGITAL WARFARE AGAINST TAIWAN

The Kansai story is just one among a great flood of manufactured falsehoods—made in China—hitting Taiwan.

The Chinese digital attacks take place particularly intensely in the run-up to presidential and parliamentary elections in Taiwan. The intention is to influence the elections in China's favor, so that political candidates—typically from the DPP—are discredited.

I talk to Puma Shen about Chinese interference and disinformation. He has a legal background and is a professor at Taiwan University. He has served as a lawyer in high-profile cases, among other things, regarding the repayment of the Nationalist Party's funds acquired during the authoritarian period, when state and party coffers partially merged. And then Puma Shen is simultaneously the co-founder of Doublethink Lab, a civil society organization that digs up and publishes examples of Chinese disinformation in Taiwan, and the founder of Kuma Academy, whose course I attended in Chapter 6. Puma is usually a teacher at Kuma in the presentation on Chinese disinformation, but he was absent, the day I attended. And after our meeting, Puma Shen decided to run for office in the parliamentary elections on 13 January 2024.

Back in January 2023, Puma arrives at our café meeting on a bicycle and in jeans with a huge hair mop. He looks more like

130

an artist than a lawyer or professor. Taiwanese people often choose English first names to make pronunciation easier for foreigners. I'm intrigued by his choice of Puma as his English first name. He took that from the clothing brand when he played basketball as a youngster. In addition, Puma also played an active role in the sunflower movement in 2013–14, while he was working on his PhD. at the University.

The digital realm is just one area in which China is trying to influence Taiwan's political life, Puma says.

China's influence in Taiwan runs wider and deeper. Among other things, Puma has investigated how China's Communist Party tries to influence Taiwanese Buddhist temples to present China in a positive light or to recommend certain political candidates to the faithful. China does this by donating money to restore or build new temples and offering the monks all-expenses-paid trips to China. However, the efforts have not been highly successful in getting Taiwan's Buddhist monks to love China, Puma can conclude from his research.

The next example of Chinese influence is from the university world. "Many professors have a close relationship with China", he explains. Puma tells me that wages are low in Taiwan and that university employees need to have many publications in print for promotion. That's where good offers from China come into play with the possibility of quick publications and to make money on textbooks (politically uncontroversial ones, naturally) for the much larger Chinese market. In return, they "promote pro-China content in their lessons," Puma explains, adding that he knows of examples of teachers who also compile lists of students who support Taiwanese independence.

Finally, Puma has discovered quite close connections between the Taiwanese mafia and China. The mafia is used to channel Chinese money into Taiwan for bribes and other purposes. But the mafia is also used in the digital realm by China, although Puma is a little cautious with his conclusions because the mafia is a dangerous opponent. However, he has observed that members of the mafia run Facebook groups, often popular ones exceeding 500,000 followers, through which Chinese disinformation circulates.

As an example, Puma cites the circulation of an anti-American story about the US buying up Taiwan's computer chips, and when the chips are safe in the US, Uncle Sam will drop support for Taiwan. "China is really good at such stories," adds Puma. They try out different conspiracy theories in closed groups and let them circulate, see what catches on, subsequently the stories can later be re-activated more widely in connection with an igniting external event.

"We find ourselves in a delicate balance because we are a country with freedom of expression," Puma points out. Taiwanese citizens are well within their right to freedom of expression to be critical of the US, but the challenge is if the public debate is infused with state-controlled propaganda from China that shouldn't influence Taiwan's political life.

I experience disinformation about Taiwan's computer chips first-hand when I search on YouTube for video material from TSMC's factory opening in the US at the end of 2022. The YouTube clip, that is promoted, seems objective enough at first, but then takes a strange turn and explains, among other falsehoods, that the Taiwanese engineers in the United States are treated inhumanely and second-rate compared to the American employees. The publisher claims to be a tech media outlet in Hong Kong and has thousands of followers.

"YouTube is problematic because it is easier to spread rumors there than on Facebook," explains Puma. Facebook already tightened up ahead of Taiwan's 2020 presidential election, actively blocking content and users identified as Chinese propagandists and who were spreading disinformation about Taiwan's election. That is why disinformation has moved to YouTube, explains Puma. The Chinese use artificial intelligence to have their "articles" read aloud and transform them into YouTube videos. From there, they re-share the videos on Facebook and with some success, because it is harder to fact-check audio-based than text-based content.

"That's the reality right now," concludes Puma. Some YouTubers who spread Chinese propaganda are Taiwanese citizens, which gives them more credibility in Taiwan, but their funding comes from China. Puma has uncovered that. "If you scan their QR code for donations, you find the Chinese services WeChat or Alipay. Strange, as Taiwanese don't use Alipay and WeChat. And you need a Chinese bank account to use WeChat".

"Not very well," is Puma's overall conclusion on how well Taiwan is tackling Chinese disinformation, even with all the awareness initiatives he personally is involved in. He worries about teenagers and the younger generation, who are more cynical and whose primary sources are YouTube and TikTok videos. "Many teenagers think that if I can watch Hollywood movies and if I can watch anime from Japan, then I can also watch videos from China." In addition, many of the young people are very skeptical of the United States. And disinformation reinforces that sentiment. An opinion poll shows that US skepticism is increasing among the Taiwanese population, especially among the younger segment.

CHINA AND TAIWAN—CENSORSHIP VERSUS OPENNESS

Together with Puma, I review the fundamental differences between China and Taiwan in the digital field. Since 2009, the Chinese authorities have enclosed the Chinese citizens behind a digital Chinese (fire-)Wall. The Chinese social media and internet that ordinary Chinese have access to, are censored and under state control. In practice, that means that when you search on the Chinese internet, you do not get the same results as we do on www. or Google, but instead they are met with blocked pages or state-controlled propaganda. Search Tiananmen massacre—no results. Dalai Lama—you get state propaganda that he is a dangerous terrorist. Taiwan's Democratic Development?—"Page not found".

It is also not possible to criticize the Communist Party and Xi Jinping on China's social media such as Weibo, Douyin (TikTok's Chinese sister app) and WeChat. The censorship is so blatant that many Chinese have started euphemistically referring to Xi Jinping as Winnie the Pooh because of a certain physical resemblance. But Winnie the Pooh is now also on the list of forbidden words. The Chinese, unless they are persistent or use illegal technical solutions as a Virtual Private Network (VPN), do not have immediate and legal access to Google, Facebook, Instagram and Twitter/X. On the other hand, China's state-controlled press, authorities and internet trolls enjoy using Twitter/X to spread their messages. There is a clear asymmetry. The Chinese authorities have cut off their own citizens from the open internet and from international social media, but use the same media for propaganda and disinformation in democratic countries. First on that list is Taiwan.

In Taiwan, the population lives in a completely different and open digital reality. Facebook and other social media are widespread, as well as the popular local app Line, which serves both as a network for chat communication and as the hub where Taiwanese book a taxi, a theater ticket and much more.

OPENNESS IN TAIWAN—A CONVERSATION WITH AUDREY TANG

The country's digital minister, Audrey Tang embodies Taiwan's digital openness. Tang also has a fan base in the LGBTQ+ community. She refers to herself as beyond classic gender definitions and is indifferent to which pronoun her interlocutors employ. When I wrote an article in 2020 featuring Audrey Tang, I used he/him, so for variation this time I use she/her.

Audrey Tang has long black hair, round owl-eyeglasses and hails from Taiwan's white hat hacker community, where you use your programming skills to help society. She masters the programming languages Perl and Haskell, but jokingly says that she dreams in JavaScript. You can find her on a popular TED-Talk. She is a smart celebrity that you find on a web search in an interesting dialogue with the equally popular Israeli historian Yuval Harari.

In 2013, Audrey Tang was active in the sunflower movement, and not long after she became what she labels as a "reverse mentor" to a Taiwanese minister, advising him on how the government should handle the digital portfolio.

In 2016, she was appointed minister without portfolio. In practice, this meant that she became the government's spokeswoman on all matters tech and digital.

In August 2022, she was appointed minister of digital affairs with her own ministry. Still, Tang continues to see herself as an outsider who happens to be in government as a link to civil society and the tech sector.

Accordingly, her most important principle is radical transparency in government. In practice that means all her meetings take place on-the-record. When we sit down together, she immediately presses the record button. Afterwards, the transcribed audio file is available on the internet. Everyone can read and hear what we talked about. Her transparency procedure turns out to be my luck during our interview, as I didn't press my record button properly on my phone.

With radical transparency, there is no need for burdensome freedom of information requests to figure out with whom and about what Audrey Tang meets. Citizens have immediate insight. From a democratic point of view, it is inspiring and more advanced than the public administration policies in many other developed democracies in Europe or in the US.

For other parts of the Taiwanese government, her openness might be a quite innovative, but for Tang it is a fundamental and value-based approach. It is also a response to China's digital closure and censorship. Openness and citizens' participation are Taiwan's defenses against the authoritarian digital threat on the other side of the Taiwan Strait. Because China is bigger and has larger resources at its disposal, the Taiwanese authorities will always fall short, if they try to match Chinese propaganda and disinformation one-on-one.

For Tang, it's about educating Taiwan's citizens digitally so that they help create a society governed by a shared belief in facts and truth. Digital media skills have been integrated into primary school teaching. Tang talks about similar courses being offered at evening schools and in other forms of lifelong learning, "because my parents' generation also needs it," she explains.

On the app Line, which is widespread in Taiwan and resembles WhatsApp, you can invite an impartial fact-checker from civil society into your family and other chat groups, so that the news story which, for example, grandma sends around that covid came out of an American laboratory, can get an unbiased check to see if it holds water or should be labelled as disinformation.

"Resilience" is Tang's reply to what she wants to achieve as digital minister. She emphasizes the need to be able to work from anywhere. People do not need an office or to be physically in Taiwan. Her own office is a tablet and a phone.

WHAT LESSONS FROM UKRAINE FOR TAIWAN'S DIGITAL DEFENSE?

I ask what lessons learned Audrey Tang draws from Russia's invasion of Ukraine.

"Uninterrupted internet connection and good journalists," is her answer.

Without both internet connectivity and factual journalism, Ukraine could not have told its story to the outside world. Tang mentions that at the beginning of the war, the Russians tried to cast doubt on what was going on with fake news and disinformation. Stories circulated that Zelenskyy had fled—an attempt by Russia to reduce Ukrainian resistance, but fortunately without much effect.

Ukraine's uninterrupted internet connectivity with the outside world—helped by Elon Musk, who activated the Starlink satellites—and good factual journalism from the English-language media Kyiv Independent, which Tang emphasizes that she read extensively, were vital for Ukraine. That goes for Taiwan too, adds Tang. Consequently, her ministry is in the process of creating additional resilience on internet access.

In the case of Taiwan, internet access is secured by individual submarine cables. Those cables could be exposed to sabotage. It is important to protect the cables, but difficult to monitor many kilometers on the seabed.

Shortly after my conversation with Audrey Tang, two Taiwanese internet cables are mysteriously cut, caused by "accidents" from Chinese civilian ships. However, the cables are not main cables to Taiwan itself, but service the Matsu Islands, which lie close to the Chinese mainland. Without a proper internet connection for Matsu's residents, it can take ten minutes just to send a text message. Matsu must survive for several months with patchwork solutions before full internet is restored.

To prevent Taiwan from suffering internet breakdowns caused by China, Taiwan is in the process of expanding its cooperation with satellite operators from democratic countries as providers. The satellites will be placed at different altitudes. Since 2007, China's military has demonstrated its capacity to precisely shoot down satellites. Taiwan's resilience consists in having several different options and suppliers, "more eggs in the basket", Audrey Tang describes the strategy.

Another protective move is to manufacture 5G networks in new mini versions led by local Taiwanese technology companies such as Pegatron and HTC. They have succeeded in producing 5G-receivers down-sized to fit in a suitcase. The mobile network itself has also become mobile. It can be carried around and connected to satellite access. No need for larger 5G reception towers which take time to install. Classic stationary towers are more vulnerable to being spotted and destroyed in a conflict.

Audrey Tang says that the fire department in Hsinchu—very fittingly the city which houses Taiwan's silicon production—has already adopted such mobile connections.

Audrey Tang also highlights Diia, the Ukrainian app and citizen engagement platform, as something Taiwan can learn from. Diia has enabled useful citizen-driven communication during the war, allowing people to receive digital public documents, report on Russian troops and war crimes, or find the nearest emergency room.

Consequently, Tang and her team are working through how the existing Taiwanese digital citizen platforms, especially the health apps that were used to deal with Covid, could hold broader opportunities—"dual-use" as she calls it—in the event of a conflict situation, allowing citizens and authorities to cooperate.

I also talk to Audrey Tang about Nancy Pelosi's visit to Taiwan in August 2022. It led to a large increase in cyber-attacks on Taiwan. Most of the attacks were relatively simple so-called DDoS, "denial of service" attacks, which can shut down websites. It happened to the Taiwanese Ministry of Foreign Affairs, whose website was put out of action. But what was novel and with greater sophistication, Tang elaborates, was that simultaneously Chinese disinformation was spread that the Taiwanese Foreign Ministry had been completely hacked. When journalists wanted to fact-check that information, the Ministry of Foreign Affairs' website was out of service. In this way, the DDoS attack appeared to be broader than it was.

Since that incident, the Taiwanese government has been preparing for similar future website blackouts combined with targeted Chinese disinformation about a societal breakdown or similar in Taiwan. The intention of the Chinese is to show that they can use digital tools to sow at a minimum doubt and at best panic in the population.

During Pelosi's visit, the only website that could not be brought down by DDoS attacks was that of the Ministry of Digital Affairs. "It wasn't down for a second," says Audrey Tang with pride. With her past as a programmer, she had added several layers of protection. She mentions several abbreviations, but as I understand it, the best protection was a decentralized network: InterPlanetary File System abbreviated IPFS. I pull the "it's-too-technical-for-me" card, so I do get an explanation I can understand and pass on. IPFS is a decentralized network of computer users worldwide who store copies of websites on their computers. It becomes impossible to hack because the copies are spread out on thousands of computers all over the world. Tang also notes with satisfaction that there were computer users in authoritarian countries who supported the ministry's website. Since then, all Taiwanese ministries have switched to that kind of user- and network-driven security system.

Global digital cooperation is a strong card for Taiwan. In cyberspace, China's power is in some areas smaller. Netizens are not concerned with—and are not constrained by—the one-China policy. Taiwan has its own national domain extension—.tw. It is thus uniquely its own country on the digital map. A TED talk with Audrey Tang passes around the globe across national borders and cannot be stopped by China invoking the one-China policy. Taiwan can connect globally in the digital area without China being able to block it—precisely because China itself has chosen to cut itself off from a good part of the global internet including American social media. There is international space for Taiwan. President Tsai

Ing-wen, for example, has millions of followers on Twitter and Instagram, where Xi Jinping is absent.

CHINA AND RUSSIA'S DIGITAL COOPERATION ON COVID AND THE UKRAINE WAR

I also receive good input on online disinformation from Poyu Tseng, a digital researcher and from Ttcat, whose full name is Wu Min-hsuan, who leads Doublethink Lab, a civil society organization that aims to combat digital misinformation and disinformation, especially from China.

One of Doublethink Lab's newer initiatives is a measurement of Chinese disinformation in over 80 countries, which the organization launched at a December 2022 conference in Berlin. Taiwanese researchers contribute their language skills and their special knowledge of China to the global prevention of Chinese disinformation. Chinese disinformation has now a global reach and has become far more aggressive in spreading false rumors on social media over recent years—also in collaboration with Russia.

Secret minutes of internal meetings uncovered by Radio Free Europe reveal that over several years China and Russia's cyber authorities have actively collaborated to spread disinformation. Russia has a longer track record of digital interference—most spectacularly in the US presidential election in 2016.

During the Covid-pandemic, both Chinese and Russian state media and representatives and bloggers spread on social media that it was in reality the United States that had invented Covid in a laboratory. In this lie, it was no longer Wuhan in China that was the epicenter of Covid.

During Russia's ongoing war against Ukraine, the Chinese state-controlled press has been spreading Russian propaganda stories about the war, including that Ukraine is populated by Nazis.

Most disturbingly, Covid and the war in Ukraine are mixed into one lie. Chinese profiles are spreading a false conspiracy theory—digitally forged in Russia—that Ukraine houses US biolabs that developed the Covid virus. The circus of disinformation comes full circle.

CHAPTER 10

Can Taiwan's freedom inspire China?

"Freedom," writes a young Taiwanese woman on an oblong white banner with the two beautiful Chinese characters. This is her message at a demonstration in support of Chinese protesters. I am in Freedom Square in downtown Taipei on a Friday evening in late November 2022.

In cities across China, just a few hundred kilometers away on the other side of the Taiwan Strait, people have taken to the streets to protest the government's strict Covid policy. Over a few wild days, the demonstrations spread across the country. Protest on this scale hadn't been seen in decades in Xi Jinping's tightly controlled society. It's the Covid restrictions that have brought people to the streets, but some protesters are also calling for more freedom of speech, and in Shanghai, protesters are calling for Xi Jinping to step down.

It is the holy trinity in China that the protesters are questioning: Covid management, the Communist Party' censorship and Xi Jinping's rule.

The protesters gather around a common symbol: a blank A4 paper, which they hold up in front of them. It is the symbol of the Chinese government's censorship. The name A4 Revolution becomes a hashtag on Western social media, which some Chinese can access using VPN connections that bypass government controls.

The demonstrations surprise most China-hands. Including me. After the first night, when the protesters are on the streets in the dark and some masked, I write with a correspondent in Shanghai who is convinced that the protesters will not return the next day in broad daylight. We are both in for a surprise. The discontent is broad-based. A large group of Chinese have the courage to demonstrate—even in the light of day, despite the police and surveillance cameras tracking and recording them.

Although China's social media is a closed bubble controlled by the Chinese government, Twitter/X, Facebook and other social media sites are overflowing with photos and videos from China. An active Chinese user @whyyoutouzhele outside of China becomes a distribution hub. He uploads on Twitter/X thousands of videos sent by users inside China, so that the testimonies are shared and can persist beyond the country's borders.

I'm following the situation from Taiwan—a completely different world when it comes to freedom of expression. One video from China that sticks with me is of a young woman walking alone down a busy street. She holds her hands out in front of her with chains on them. Duct tape is symbolically placed over her mouth, and she holds a sheet of white A4 paper in front of her.

She reminds me of the brave Iranian women who also fearlessly walk the streets without their head coverings and defy the regime.

In Chinese history, she reminds me of the unidentified man in the white shirt who stopped a tank in Tiananmen Square during the 1989 student uprising in Beijing. Even with over three decades between them, the two people share a digital destiny. Their stories don't exist on the Chinese internet. They have been edited out. Even foreign journalists in China have been unable to find out the woman's fate.

The Chinese authorities are quickly showing how effective their electronic censorship is, and even outside of China's cyber control zone they are taking action. On Twitter/X, electronic searches for the hashtag A4 revolution are flooded with advertisements and often sexual diversionary content inserted in huge quantities by Chinese state-paid cyber trolls to drown the protesters' messages.

Within China, the controls are even more subtle. Chinese protesters have photos automatically deleted—even directly without their consent—on their private phones. "You weren't there," is the message from China's electronic Big Brother. Xi Jinping never publicly acknowledges that demonstrations even took place. In the outside world, our memories are also short when images and testimonies are no longer flowing out. Only a few diligent foreign journalists in China try to follow the fates of the A4 protesters, many of whom have subsequently been arrested or disappeared without trace.

Shortly after, the A4 revolution has been electronically wiped out inside China, but with testimonies preserved on the free internet outside of China, such as in Taiwan, where it is possible to speak freely and demonstrate.

Still, the protesters might have had an effect. At least, the Chinese government reverses course after the demonstrations and rapidly lifts the covid restrictions. On this front, it shows that protests deliver results even in a closed China.

At one of the ongoing support demonstrations for the A4 revolution in Taipei's Freedom Square, which I attend, I also meet students from China who are staying in Taiwan. Not all

Chinese students abroad are nationalists or Communist Party supporters.

But even abroad, like here in Taiwan, it's not easy to be Chinese and critical of the regime, if you want to return to China or don't want to bring negative consequences to your family. That's why Chinese students wear masks and appear anonymously, especially when they are interviewed by the international press covering the support demonstrations in Taiwan.

At support demonstrations in Taipei, I also meet participants with flags from other oppressed groups. The black Hong Kong banner is raised, and I note the colorful Tibetan sun flag. I also spot a green flag for the Uighurs, the oppressed Muslim minority from Xinjiang. In Taipei, there is space for them to all have their say. I ask a young female Taiwanese organizer why she spends her time doing this: "I am a human being on this earth, and so are all the people we are protesting for. We all have the right to be here."

In contrast, I also bump into a couple of young girls 50 meters away from the demonstration. They are busy with their own show: shooting a dance video for TikTok. My brief conversation with them reveals that their interest is in getting a lot of likes, while the human rights situation in China is a distant thing.

LIGHTS OUT FOR HONG KONG'S LIBERTY

For many years, Hong Kong played the role of a territory with freedom of press and speech within China. It was in Hong Kong's Victoria Square that every year on the evening of June 4, thousands of Hong Kong citizens would gather with candles to remember the students killed in Tiananmen Square in

Beijing during the 1989 student uprising. In the rest of China, June 4 is strictly censored. The censorship is so pervasive that younger generations of Chinese inhabit a people's republic of amnesia. They have never even heard of the student uprising that took place in the center of Beijing in 1989.

In Hong Kong, too, the vigil is now over. The Communist Party fundamentally changed the territory's future when they introduced the National Security Law in 2020. This law makes it possible to prosecute democracy activists in Hong Kong and severely restrict freedom of expression. On June 4, 2023, the few who were present were arrested. Hong Kong's free media has also been smashed. The founder of the free news media Apple Daily, Jimmy Lai, is imprisoned and persecuted. His media company is being dissolved.

Hong Kong has dropped from 80th to 148th place in Reporters Without Borders' press freedom assessment from 2021 to 2022, the biggest drop ever recorded. And in that sense too Hong Kong is getting closer to mainland-China, which ranks as the fifth worst country in the world for press freedom (175th out of 180).

Members of Hong Kong's democracy movement are either in prison or scattered around the world as political refugees, especially in the UK. At the annual Copenhagen Democracy Summit, we have regularly had democracy advocates and former elected officials from Hong Kong on the speaker list. This includes Joshua Wong, who is currently in prison. Nathan Law, who is currently in exile. And at the Copenhagen Democracy Summit in May 2023 Joey Sieu was on stage. In December 2023, she got a 1 million Hong Kong dollars bounty on her from the Hong Kong authorities. At the Copenhagen Democracy Summit, we will continue to be a gathering place for exiled Hong Kongers.

At the summit in May 2023, Jens Galschiøt, the Danish artist, participated with his work The Pillar of Shame. It is a sculpture dedicated to the Tiananmen victims. The statue stood for 15 years at Hong Kong University. It has now been removed. Even though our event takes place on Danish soil, as the organizers of the summit, we can be prosecuted in Hong Kong, as the national security legislation not only covers the territory of Hong Kong, but has a so-called extraterritorial provision, so acts committed abroad are also covered.

We saw this on Danish soil when the then members of parliament Uffe Elbæk and Katarina Ammitzbøll invited Hong Kong politician Ted Hui to Denmark in the fall of 2020. Hong Kong authorities threatened to issue an international arrest warrant for the two Danish MPs! This is an example of China's long arm into other countries and their efforts to stifle free debate far beyond the borders of the Middle Kingdom. From Copenhagen, Ted Hui went into exile and is now in Australia.

In the 2020 presidential election campaign in Taiwan, China's repression of Hong Kong played a crucial role in President Tsai Ing-wen's re-election. She voiced her clear support for Hong Kong's protesters and the democracy movement. The repression of Hong Kong also meant that Beijing's "one-country-two-systems", which officially applies to Hong Kong, was unmasked as a hollow propaganda tool. It is the same model of peaceful "reunification" offered by the Chinese Communist Party to Taiwan. But in practice, the Hong Kong process has shown that the power of the Chinese Communist Party reigns supreme.

The 2020 presidential candidate of the Nationalist Party, Han Kuo-yu, who stood for closer economic relations with China, struggled to find an answer to Hong Kong's situation and China's aggressive behavior. This was a contributing factor in his election loss to Tsai Ing-wen. In January 2024, Hong Kong plays a minor role in Taiwan's elections.

THE HARD EXILE FROM HONG KONG

During my time in Taiwan, I meet up with activists from Hong Kong who have continued their work in Taiwan. Many fled here because Taiwan is close by and because it remains a free democratic society.

To my surprise, I meet an old acquaintance from Hong Kong. Let's just call him Freddy, as he is now trying to live a different life far away from the "revolution of our time", which was the slogan of the Hong Kong protesters.

We met during the large demonstrations and clashes with the police in 2019 in Hong Kong. At the time, he was advocating for European countries to enforce sanctions against the Hong Kong authorities in response to police brutality against the protesters. I rediscover a video on WhatsApp that Freddy sent me showing footage of a police officer shooting a protester at point-blank range. Those images went around the world at the time.

At the time, Freddy gave me the impression that he personally was in the front line of the demonstrations and the street battles against the Hong Kong police, who were increasingly using heavy violence against the protesters.

In 2019, he gave me a Hong Kong support T-shirt that with the inscription "Defend and destroy". It depicted a protester wearing a yellow hard hat and a gas mask. Even then, the T-shirt struck me as too militant for me, so I never wore it. But on a whim, I took it with me in my suitcase for my stay in Taiwan.

I haven't had any contact with Freddy since 2020. In fact, I thought he was either in jail (which is why I didn't send messages, even on encrypted media, in case his phone had ended up in police custody) or at worst had died in the Hong Kong street fighting around the university.

It is therefore a pleasant surprise to find out that Freddy is both alive and well in Taipei. We agree to meet for dinner.

It's a surprising conversation. I quickly realize that Freddy has a quite different take on things today. He refers to the Hong Kong revolution as "romantic". His revolutionary streak has faded.

He has found a job in Taiwan and claims to be happy with his new life. His message to other Hong Kongers in exile is to create a new life without nostalgia. I've brought the Hong Kong T-shirt, he offered me, to dinner and propose to give it back to him. "No thanks," even though he tells me that he has lost all his things from Hong Kong.

I leave the dinner puzzled. I did not meet a revolutionary in exile, but a man who has very quickly and pragmatically adapted to a completely different life. Of course, I can't rule out the possibility that even in free Taiwan, Freddy may be anxious about Chinese reprisals and is adapting to a world where China's repressive capacity extends far beyond Hong Kong.

I also get in touch with several other Hong Kongers in Taiwan. One of them, let's call her Reese, because she also wants to remain anonymous as her family still lives in Hong Kong and could face reprisals from the authorities, runs a small NGO, which I visit in humble premises.

The organization helps Hong Kongers in Taiwan but is also part of a global Hong Kong exile community. They publish a magazine to keep the spirit of freedom and democracy alive outside of Hong Kong. The first time we meet, we go to the movies and watch a movie about the Hong Kong revolution. That kind of movie is now impossible to watch in Hong Kong, and in the rest of China of course. We can in Taiwan.

Another time we meet, Reese is frustrated because her Taiwanese landlord has terminated the lease at short notice because he won't house their political activities. It reflects the duality that some Hong Kongers face even in free Taiwan.

Some of the sympathy from the Taiwanese in 2020 has evaporated now that the Hong Kongers need to be integrated into a new life in Taiwan. The immigration and especially the citizenship process is slow and lengthy, even for Hong Kongers. There is no clear process for political refugees. They are bureaucratically referred to as "special cases". It takes a minimum of five years to obtain citizenship.

Even in free Taiwan, exile from Hong Kong is not an easy future. Several Hong Kongers also cite the fear that one day they will have to move on if China invades Taiwan. Their exile status feels permanent.

CHINA-DEMOCRATIC FORCES IN TAIWAN

In Taiwan, I connect with Wang Dan, one of the most active student leaders from the 1989 student uprising. There is an iconic photo of him from 1989 in international newspapers, where he speaks to the assembled protesters at Tiananmen Square. In the background is the Forbidden City and the large portrait of Mao hanging above the entrance gate. Wang Dan wear large glasses and thick, black bowl-cut hair; his look at the time. When we meet in Taipei, his hair remains black but crew-cut short and his glasses are gone—undoubtedly replaced by contact lenses.

On June 4, 1989, the Chinese regime deployed the military into Tiananmen Square and shot down the protesters. Wang Dan, who was on Beijing's most wanted list, was imprisoned until 1998. After that he went into exile in the United States, received an education and got new opportunities, but remains active for democratic change in China. In recent years, he has also taught at Taiwanese universities.

I want to hear his views about the A4 demonstrations. Dan admits that as a long-time Chinese dissident, he too was surprised by the demonstrations and their scale. "It illustrates that we basically don't know what the Chinese people are thinking because they are suppressed and censored. Wang Dan believes that we are facing a period of great uncertainty about what is going to happen in China. On the surface, there is Xi Jinping's strongman rule, but change can come suddenly and unexpectedly. Therefore, he emphasizes, the Chinese youth is the future. We need to work with them—inside and outside China. Such contacts are difficult because the regime actively blocks contacts, but we must try anyway, Wang concludes.

I also meet with Li Ming-che, a Taiwanese who was held in a Chinese prison for several years until spring 2022. He is one of the few democracy activists that Congresswoman Nancy Pelosi met with during her visit in August 2022. Li's crime—in the eyes of the Chinese system—was to explain to ordinary Chinese people how Taiwanese democracy works. Due to international pressure, Li explains to me, his trial in China was conducted in open court. It exposed the absurdity of the charges against him. Among other things, texts he had written on Facebook while he was outside of China were presented in court as part of the charges. Despite his imprisonment, Li's belief that fighting for rights in China is worthwhile is unshaken.

Soft pop tones play from the stage. The audience waves color-changing lightsabers in their hands. I'm at a Kimberley Chen concert in Taipei. But what does pop music have to do with China and freedom of expression? Actually, quite a lot.

Kimberley Chen, who is Australian-Taiwanese, sings in Mandarin. It's called Mando-pop, like K-pop from Korea. Her songs are heard by millions—even in China. Or they were in the past. In 2021, she released a song called "Fragile", which could be construed as critical of Xi Jinping, but it was by no means an actual protest song. For example, the color pink, which is associated with Xi Jinping's fans in China (referred to as the little pinkies), was used consistently in the music video. A quick check on YouTube shows that over 66 million people have listened to the song.

The situation is different in China. Censorship moved in. Kimberley's profiles on Chinese social media were deleted. She was wiped digitally, as only the Chinese cyber authorities can do.

I heard about the censorship story, so I contacted Kimberley and invited her to Denmark. On June 9, 2022, she took the stage at Skuespilhuset in Copenhagen and sang the banned song at the Copenhagen Democracy Summit.

In Taiwan, I talk to one of Kimberley's managers, who tells me that the Chinese market is big and attractive, but that Taiwanese singers are increasingly staying away precisely because Kimberley's case, gives second thoughts. A singer can suddenly be censored. No one knows exactly where the boundaries are of what you can sing until China's censorship kicks in.

It is also in the world of music and art that the battle for freedom of expression with authoritarian China takes place.

Under the authoritarian rule of Chiang Kai-shek and later his son in Taiwan, freedom of speech was restricted until the late 1980s. In that period, Taiwanese advocates like magazine publisher Nylon Cheng (with the motto 100% free speech) fought to expand the scope of what could be written in Taiwan.

Today, Taiwan's press is free and unruly—as it should be in a democracy. Taiwan is ranked number 38 on the Reporters Without Borders classification. This is 137 places better than China.

In recent years, the foreign press has moved to Taiwan. This is because China has become more closed and has expelled international journalists because they cannot tolerate their critical coverage of conditions in China. This means that internationally recognized China journalists like the New York Times' Chris Buckley, who I met in the 10s during visits to Beijing, arrived in Taiwan at the end of 2022.

Hong Kong used to be a bastion of free speech where reporters could cover China from. With the new restrictions, Hong Kong journalists are also moving on to Taiwan, where journalists are not harassed, and freedom of speech and press is intact.

This is also seen in the Danish press. Previously, all Danish journalists were accredited in China. In 2022, the first Danish correspondent based in Taiwan arrived from Politiken. Berlingske followed suit with a correspondent in the summer of 2023.

It may turn out to be a disservice that China has scared international journalists out of China. For Taiwan, at least, the benefit is that more people around the globe will learn about the country's unique history as more journalists cover China and Asia from Taiwan.

Taiwan's freedoms are now a foundation of the country's political life.

Since Taiwan harbors Chinese and Hong Kong dissidents and gives them a voice, the Beijing regime sees Taiwan's freedom as a threat to its authoritarian rule.

It was for the same reason that the regime saw it as imperative to crush Hong Kong's democracy movement—it was incompatible with the Communist Party's monopoly on power.

The Chinese government tells us that a Western-inspired democracy is incompatible with Chinese tradition. The Chinese people need a strong and centralized system, we are told by spokespersons of the Chinese Communist Party.

Taiwan's free way of life dispels that narrative. I see it as a trump card in Taiwan's battle with China that Taiwan is living proof that people of Chinese descent—like all other people around the globe—thrive in a free society.

A young Taiwanese woman I meet in Taipei wants me to predict what will happen to Taiwan in 2040. Naturally, I don't know. However, I reply that I imagine that Taiwan will still be a free democracy in 2040. And that by 2040, China may also have become a democracy that no longer threatens its neighbors. This answer fills her with optimism for the future, she replies. I hope for her sake and for the people of both Taiwan and China that this could turn out to be their future.

CHAPTER 11

The battle for Taiwan— concluding observations

I don't expect to shake hands with Xi Jinping again. Since the handshake in 2016, I have shaken hands with Hong Kong activists like Nathan Law, Joey Sieu, Ted Hui, Chinese dissidents like Wang Dan and Yang Jianli, and in the making of this book with Taiwan's political leadership, who are seen as dangerous separatists by China.

Getting on the wrong side of the Chinese Communist Party can come at great personal cost. In December 2018, China unjustly imprisoned two Canadians, Michael Kovrig and Michael Spavor, for 1,019 days. Michael Kovrig was a former Canadian diplomat in China and now at International Crisis Group, the think tank. Since his release, I have had the pleasure of meeting him at conferences outside China on China.

I would like to live in a more peaceful world where I could continue to travel into China, but that is not the world vision that Xi Jinping's autocratic leadership stands for.

WHEN COULD WAR COME?—THE FATEFUL
YEARS AHEAD

2024, 2025, 2027, 2035, 2049. As I write this book, the media
is abuzz with possible dates for a Chinese attack on Taiwan.

War worries are reinforced by the war in Ukraine and the
brutish awakening triggered by Putin's invasion. Destructive
great power war is again a possibility—also in an interdepen-
dent trade-globalized world—and also against Taiwan.

2024 marks the election year. Taiwan elections are in January and the country changes its president in May 2024. The
US holds presidential elections in November 2024 and inau-
gurates the newly elected president in January 2025.

What is certain in 2024 is that China will react outwardly
to Taiwan's election. That is the base line. Especially if the DPP
candidate, the current vice president, Lai Ching-te is elected.
China will seize the opportunity to as a minimum threaten
militarily and put increased economic and cyber pressure on
Taiwan.

If Hou Yu-ih from KMT wins the 2024 election, it could
spell more economic cooperation with China, at least in the
short term. But even in that case, it could be a short honey-
moon period. A full return to the economic embrace of Ma
Ying-jeou, the last KMT president elected in 2008, is not likely
either. Times have changed. The KMT leadership is also aware
of the popular resistance in Taiwan to wide-ranging economic
cooperation with China.

In January 2025, a newly elected president will be inaugu-
rated in Washington DC. China can use the uncertain months
of the election period to test both the US and Taiwan's new
leadership—also militarily. A cleverly executed Chinese naval quarantine of Taiwan employing primarily civilian means
could be a difficult test for a new US administration.

2027 is the year Xi Jinping has announced that his military must be ready for a Taiwan invasion. How much to read into that demand is uncertain but war probability is intensified. It is also the year when Xi Jinping will have to renew his mandate as leader of the Communist Party and thus of China.

Military capabilities are dynamic and relative quantities that depend on the capabilities of the counterpart. Both Taiwan and the US are aware that China's military is aiming for 2027, so both countries are strengthening their respective military capabilities, skewing China's calculations. "China's military has given us their time horizon. We have to stay ahead all the time, so it pushes their target date," a US official responsible for China in the US Department of Defense explains it to me.

2035 is another possible year marker for when China could be ready to try and seize Taiwan. Admiral Chen points out that year to me. He emphasizes that by then, China will have completed extensive road and land connections and, not least, secured overland energy supplies into China. The Ukraine war is accelerating that development. China is gaining better access to cheap energy from Russia, which is fast-tracking its pipelines eastwards after the clash with Europe over Ukraine.

By 2035 at the latest, China will no longer be vulnerable on energy security or that the US Navy—in a conflict situation— could block maritime access for Chinese energy supplies through the Strait of Malacca in the south and in the north through the Taiwan-Japan Strait. Admiral Chen believes that a secure energy supply is a crucial parameter for China to be able to fight, endure and win against the US.

Finally, there is the year 2049. This is the year the People's Republic of China celebrates 100 years on the world stage. By 2049, the unified China should lead the world. Any future communist leader—Xi Jinping will also be close to 100 years old himself, so he's expectedly retired—will have incorporated Taiwan by then. The final piece in the Chinese puzzle after Hong Kong's subjugation. As Xi Jinping has said, the Taiwan issue is not one that can keep being pushed from "generation to generation".

WATCH OUT: THE WARNING SIGNS OF CONFLICT

China is the expected aggressor in a military conflict, but there are dynamics in both the US and Taiwan that could spark conflict. I'm providing some markers for chip investors, war researchers and all of us ordinary citizens to keep an eye on.

From the US side, watch out for moves to officially recognize Taiwan. In the Republican Party, there are voices in favor of the US changing its policy and recognizing Taiwan as independent. Mike Pompeo, the former US Secretary of State under Donald Trump, takes such a line. Trump, however, seems more pragmatic, and revelations from his time in office show that he was willing to "sell" Taiwan to China if he could get a better trade deal for the US. If Trump returns, it could be fateful for Taiwan. Without US military support against China, Taiwan would probably be the world's loneliest democracy. That's one extreme.

At the other extreme, and a dangerous cocktail for Taiwan as well, is a United States that declares its support for an independent Taiwan, but has not first secured its military superiority to deter China, which would actually be compelled to start a war if their assessment was that the US administration has completely abandoned the one-China policy. Therefore, it is important to keep an eye on what is happening with Taiwan policy in the US and especially within the Republican Party.

In Taiwan, watch out for political moves that push Taiwan towards further independence, which could fuel the war machine on the mainland. However, there are no serious political forces left in Taiwan that want to launch a referendum on independence under the name Taiwan. Presidential frontrunner Lai Ching-te has stated that he seeks the status quo and peace not unexpected independence moves.

In China, we need a modern-day Sigmund Freud to psychoanalyze Xi Jinping's dictatorial brain. Xi's so-called Chinese dream is to create a Chinese motherland, whose mission and territorial extent is not complete until Taiwan is incorporated. The rational analysis of Xi Jinping's options would be to hold off on a military attack.

Ukraine has shown that it is not easy to defeat even a much smaller opponent militarily if the will to fight is present in the population. The superpower USA has also tried that in Vietnam and other military conflicts.

The People's Republic of China's attack on Taiwan could end in military stalemate and economic devastation, but without securing a clear Chinese victory. If Xi initiated a conflict with Taiwan and lost, it could also lead to Xi Jinping's bastion of power being challenged on the home front by the military or other Communist Party leaders. A conflict is thus also a risk for him personally if it leads to anything other than unqualified military success.

The less risk-averse strategy on Xi's part would be to continue the diplomatic and economic anaconda strategy that is slowly sucking the oxygen out of Taiwan's interactions with the outside world. Coupled with greatly increased military pressure. Then China can simply continue to wait for a future Taiwanese leader under pressure to be willing to sign some kind of peace treaty that subjects Taiwan to China's supremacy.

After all, winning the battle for Taiwan without war remains the most desirable Chinese scenario. That seems to be why Xi Jinping has put his chief ideologue Wang Huning in charge of the Taiwan-file. Give it one last chance if China could win without firing a shot.

But all these considerations presuppose that Xi Jinping sees the world through rational glasses. As Taiwanese Foreign Minister Joseph Wu tells me with some doubt in his voice: "I'm not sure the Chinese leaders are rational enough in thinking about that."

Instability within China could upset Xi's calculus. China's population growth peaked in 2022 and the country is ageing, with all that entails in terms of elder burden and pension savings, while average income remains low. Economically, China hasn't recovered to the same strength post-Covid either. Youth unemployment is rampant. War can be used to unite the nation. Just as Putin did when he took Crimea in 2014 and partially continues to do so with the Ukraine invasion.

Another danger in an authoritarian system is the creation of an echo chamber of followership around the leader. This is especially true in the military top, where Xi has secured loyalty through purges. Therefore, the risk is that the generals in 2027 will simply tell Xi Jinping what they know he wants to hear: "We are ready to take Taiwan, General Secretary Xi."

This scenario is reminiscent of Putin's interactions with his military leaders, where Putin believed that after years of rearmament, his military forces were in good shape for a quick invasion of Ukraine in 2022. Instead, many of the Russian military investments had disappeared into corruption.

We won't get into Xi Jinping's brain, but we can take seriously his publicly stated intention to use all means—including military—to secure Taiwan. We should listen to—and act on—that publicly declared intention. We would move from naive to foolish if we did not learn from the Putin experience. And we should take note of the reality that Chinese planes and navy are circling closer to Taiwan day by day. It is clearly China that is upsetting the status quo in the Taiwan Strait and exercising war scenarios.

EASTERN EUROPE AT THE FOREFRONT OF THE EU'S DEFENSE OF TAIWAN'S DEMOCRACY

Although both Danish and European policy is anchored in the One China policy, which recognizes the People's Republic of China, there is room for maneuver to further support Taiwan.

Putin's attack on Ukraine certainly shows that we in European countries did not do enough to deter an autocracy's attack on a neighboring democracy. In both Europe and Asia, the question is what kind of world order we want to live in. Everyone wants peace, but not on the aggressor's terms.

Therefore, European politicians should be much clearer and give unequivocal support to Taiwan's ability to maintain its democratic system and free way of life. This should be their value-based starting point. Especially at a time when Taiwan is globally at the top of democratic rankings and when China has become more authoritarian with no prospect of improvement.

The two countries are clearly divided into freedom and dictatorship. Democracy and autocracy. Choosing between the two countries requires freedom-minded politicians who have the courage to speak out to their voters and to China.

In Europe, these leaders are found in Eastern Europe. Lithuania's Prime Minister Symonité and Foreign Minister Landsbergis led the way, willing to risk the country's entire China trade to increase cooperation with Taiwan in 2021. Slovakia and the Czech Republic have also increased their cooperation with Taiwan.

The big step towards a rapprochement with Taiwan came with Czech President Petr Pavel. Elected in January 2023, he immediately did something unprecedented from a European leader. He spoke with Tsai Ing-wen. China condemned the conversation and expressed dismay that their basic norm, the One China principle, had been violated. Pavel held firm.

Pavel's example should set the standard for the EU's Taiwan policy, so that everyone is clearer about the right to free trade and interaction with Taiwan. It should not be the autocracy in Beijing that determines and sets the bar for European politicians' right to interact with Taiwan's elected politicians. That message was also delivered by former British Prime Minister Liz Truss when she visited Taiwan in May 2023 as the first former Prime Minister since Margaret Thatcher.

On the other side is, for example, French President Emmanuel Macron, who went to China on a state visit in April 2023. He was given pomp and circumstance by Xi Jinping, but when it came to discussing Taiwan, Macron did not bring up the subject himself, even though China announced renewed military exercises around Taiwan in response to Tsai Ing-wen's meeting in the US with Kevin McCarthy. In an interview with Politico in connection with the China visit, Macron positioned Europe as neutral in a conflict between China and the US over Taiwan.

I disagree with that vision. You cannot be neutral when it comes to the frontline of freedom. Macron should have learned from his futile diplomatic efforts with Putin over Ukraine that with dictators, only military and economic deterrence has an effect, not diplomatic coffee talk. Macron appears with what can be called preemptive obedience. China doesn't even need to raise its voice. Others fall into line in advance. Macron's statements also received American reactions. Republican Senator Marco Rubio from Florida responded to Macron that Europe can take care of Ukraine and the US will take care of Taiwan. This is not a desirable scenario or a good division of labor, as the US contributes significantly to Ukraine's defense.

On this issue, we, Europeans should orient ourselves towards Pavel rather than Macron.

EUROPE'S PEACE CONTRIBUTION: DETER CHINA WITH ECONOMIC SANCTIONS

In the event of a Taiwan war, it would be the US and expectedly its Asian ally, Japan, who would play the primary military role.

I have no illusions that Europe—apart from France and the UK to a lesser extent—will be able to play a major military role in the Taiwan Strait.

For the EU, it's about helping to prevent war, and here we have power to add from economics and sanctions.

European governments, individually and together in the EU, must make it clear to China's leadership that further military escalation against Taiwan can and will be met with sanctions, just as it has been in Russia's case. This must be the message to Xi Jinping from the EU and NATO member states. It is preventive deterrence.

Our companies must be encouraged to leave China if China's military attacks Taiwan, thus abandoning a pillar of the civilized world.

Some will argue that sanctioning China could be very costly for us, much more costly than our withdrawal from Russia after February 2022. This is true.

But it can prove just as costly to try to find an unsustainable neutral position.

In the event of a war in the Taiwan Strait, Europeans would quickly feel the full economic impact anyway. The negative effects on the world economy due to Taiwan's computer chips would hit us all when we run out of new iPhones and other electronics that power our everyday and working lives.

And a great power game of sanctions and economic muscle would emerge between the US and China. Europeans would also be forced to take a stand—and to choose sides. It is important to prepare soberly for this scenario, regardless of your attitude towards the value-political dimension of standing up for Taiwan.

The US President would call the European capitals and expect allied support, at a minimum with economic sanctions against China. This is the most relevant asset NATO allies have to offer to support Taiwan and the US.

China would try the same thing in reverse, using its economic muscle and market access to pressure European countries to remain neutral in the conflict.

In other words, there is no mouse hole big enough for Europeans to crawl into and avoid the economic consequences.

Against this backdrop, the EU and member states should make it clear to businesses that we are in a new world. In that world, trade with China has a significantly increased risk premium. And in that world, Taiwan's fate as a democracy and free society matters to us all.

"There is no point in hiding under the bed and hoping for the storm to pass," writes Foreign Minister Lars Løkke Rasmussen in May 2023 in the foreword to the Danish government's foreign policy strategy. But there is not a word about Taiwan and the possible conflict out there in the strategy. In that regard, Danish foreign policy does try to hide under the bed.

Instead, the German Green Foreign Minister, Annalena Baerbock, sends this warning signal already in September 2022 in a speech with pointed words to German industry. "Just crossing our fingers and thinking that things will probably not be so bad with these autocratic regimes is a mistake we cannot afford to make a second time," says the Foreign Minister, adding that she is thinking of China. This message should be repeated in European capitals.

It is especially in the 16 years (2005–21) under Chancellor Merkel that German business has moved massively into China which drives the EU's trade with China. Germany accounts for almost half of the EU's exports to the Middle Kingdom. Cars, machinery and chemicals are Germany's best-selling exports. In 2012, I wrote a report and an article in the Financial Times that Germany's increasing economic dependence on China would lead to negative strategic consequences for the transatlantic alliance and for European unity. That analysis still holds true. But now there is an urgency to correct the economic imbalance and dependency for Germany, which at least the Green members of the German government are concerned about.

We need to make sure that the dependency on Russian gas that Europe built up is not repeated in our trade with China. In fact, we're behind. China dominates supplies to Europe in new green technologies such as solar cells and batteries for electric vehicles. The European dependency is particularly evident in the processing of raw materials and most acutely in the so-called rare earths, a collective term for a number of minerals, where China dominates the European supply chain with up to 98 percent of the specific earths that are indispensable for magnets in electric motors and generators.

This requires us to take a hard look at mining in Europe. And here the Kingdom of Denmark has something to offer. There are raw materials and particularly rare earths in Greenland. It should be a priority, in cooperation with the Greenlandic government, to invest in this together. Such mining would be a significant Greenlandic-Danish contribution to supplying the free world with minerals to ensure the continued green transition.

Together in the EU and among other democratic countries, we need to create our own internal supply chains that reduce dependency on China. I'm not thinking that we should stop buying bicycle tubes from Chinese manufacturers. But we need new supply chains for sensitive technology, critical infrastructure and access to and processing of raw materials. This doesn't mean we decouple from China and stop trading tomorrow, but it does mean we take a critical look at our supply chains.

This due diligence is also exactly what European Commission President Ursula von der Leyen proposed in a speech on China relations in early April 2023. "De-risking," she labels it.

In some ways, it will be a more expensive and uncertain world we will live in. Globalization in the carefree version, as we have known it for two decades after China's entry into the World Trade Organization, is not coming back. The increasingly divided world between the US and China and between democracies and autocracies does not mean an unequivocal goodbye to globalized free trade. It is merely a farewell to naive economic dependence on autocracies.

But there are certainly new free trade opportunities too. I predict that over the coming years, we will shift our trade patterns to support our alliance and values. That is, ensuring more free trade between free nations. Within the framework of President Biden's Democracy Summit, attended by over 100 countries in March 2023, cooperation can be expanded between emerging democracies in Africa, Asia (where the majority of the world's people living in democracies reside), South and Central America.

We should look to say Botswana, Uruguay, Ghana, Brazil, Indonesia and many other democracies. In these countries, the seeds can be sown for supply chains among democratic countries, where Taiwan should also be included. European trade policy should reflect that.

One thing is certain. The battle for Taiwan will play a crucial role in our geopolitics, our economic prosperity and our compass of values for years to come.

Afterword

Thanks to Sebastian Stryhn Kjeldtoft for great company and insightful discussions in Taipei.

A big thank you to Anita Chang for helping me with Chinese and Taiwanese translation. It was a pleasure to attend the self-defense course together and meet with the Taiwanese volunteers in Ukraine.

Emily Y. Wu invited me to exciting cultural events throughout my eight weeks—a nice change from my narrow focus on geopolitics. This and the conversations with Emily gave me a better insight into Taiwanese society.

Thanks to James Holtum for proof-reading. All errors remain mine.

Thanks to Felix, my son, for reading along chapter by chapter when I was stuck in cold winter months back in Denmark, where my desire to write was quite chilled. We share a fascination of Taiwan where he studied.

Thanks to Kristin, my wife, and my son Victor for taking good care of each other and the dogs while I was in Taiwan. Kristin's visit over the New Year provided a wonderful break and the opportunity to visit the beaches on the south coast of the island together.

Thank you to the Taiwan Foundation for Democracy and staff, who were open to providing a vacant office, even though

I arrived self-arranged and outside the usual time frame for visiting guest researchers.

Thank you to Anders Fogh Rasmussen for inspiring me as a beacon of values. I appreciate our cooperation in the Alliance of Democracies Foundation and especially our visit to Taiwan in January, which is also included in this book.

Freedom is not free.

ABOUT THE AUTHOR

Jonas Parello-Plesner is Executive Director of The Alliance of Democracies Foundation, a private foundation dedicated to strengthening cooperation among democracies world-wide, which hosts the annual Copenhagen Democracy Summit. The Foundation is founded and chaired by former NATO Secretary General Anders Fogh Rasmussen.

Jonas Parello-Plesner has a background as a Danish diplomat with a focus on China and Taiwan. He was most recently Head of Department for Foreign Policy at the Danish Embassy in Washington, D.C. 2013–2017.

He has also worked as a Senior China Fellow for international think tanks in Washington, Brussels and London. He writes for Danish and international media. In 2015 he published the book "China's Strong Arm—Protecting Citizens and Assets Abroad" (Routledge).

www.ingramcontent.com/pod-product-compliance
Lightning Source LLC
Chambersburg PA
CBHW070936260726
48661CB00003B/1015